COPING WITH

A Dysfunctional Family

Paul M. Taylor and Diane B. Taylor

THE ROSEN PUBLISHING GROUP, INC./NEW YORK

COPING

W I T H

A

Dysfunctional

Family

Paul M. Taylor and Diane B. Taylor

THE ROSEN PUBLISHING GROUP, INC./NEW YORK

Published in 1990 by The Rosen Publishing Group
29 East 21st Street, New York, NY 10010

First Edition

Manufactured in the United States of America

Library of Congress Cataloging-In Publication Data

Taylor, P. M. (Paul Michael)
   Coping with a dysfunctional family / P.M. Taylor and D.B. Taylor
   1st ed.
     p.   cm.
   Includes bibliographical references and index.
   Summary: Examines various dysfunctional family scenarios,
including situations of drug abuse, alcohol abuse, neglect, and sexual
abuse. Offers advice, resource lists, and hotline numbers to teens
looking for help..
   ISBN 0-8239-1180-2
   1. Problem families--United States--Juvenile literature. 2.
Teenagers--United States--Life skills guides--Juvenile literature.
[1. Family problems. 2. Life skills.] I. Taylor, D. B. (Diane Bosley)
II. Title
   HV699.T39   1990
   362.82'024055--dc20   90-36475
                               CIP
                               AC

A B O U T   T H E   A U T H O R ◇

Both Diane Bosley Taylor and Paul Michael Taylor graduated from Michigan State University and did their postgraduate work together at Western Michigan University. Diane has taught both mainstream and remedial classes in middle school, high school, and adult education. She is currently pursuing an additional degree. Paul has taught elementary school, and worked with high school students in extracurricular programs. He currently works as a critical care nurse in a regional trauma center.

Contents

Introduction

The family unit in our culture has been seriously eroded by drugs, by alcohol, and by abuse in various forms. Teens and younger children are confused and hurt. The end result is always the same—pain. Suppressing the tears, holding in the anger, feeling self-criticism and doubt, all are symptoms of a larger disease called the dysfunctional family.

We recently spoke with the author of a book about children of alcoholics. When asked if he had taken a course or joined a group and interviewed people to do research for the book, he said, "I don't need to take a course—I lived it." We are not so self-righteous as to believe that because we too "lived it" we know and understand what has happened to others. Some of the episodes in this book happened to us personally. Some are stories of the many people we have talked with about their childhood experiences. But all the stories are true in that they are based on real people. Sometimes the sex of the character has been changed. Sometimes the location or age is different. Always the names have been changed to protect privacy. In a hospital setting and a school setting we have interviewed countless people whose lives have been touched in some way by a dysfunctional family.

The subject of dysfunctional families is too large to handle, so we have narrowed it down to five categories: (1) alcohol abuse; (2) drug abuse; (3) physical and verbal abuse; (4) sexual abuse; and (5) emotional neglect.

1

We hope that after reading the book you will see that you are not alone and that there are specific actions you can take to bring about change in your life. Read all you can on the subject. Take a course. Talk to others. We are all "living it."

CHAPTER ◇ 1

What Is a Family?

A dysfunctional family is one that's not working. You know something is wrong at home. Some days you're sure it's your parents' fault, some days you are afraid it might be all your fault.

A real family is more than a mom, dad, and two kids living in a house. A family is a home where the adults have the responsibility to provide shelter, guidance, and love to their children. It can be a stepfamily or extended to include aunts, uncles, or grandparents. But a family that works gives support to everyone in the home. It allows children to grow safely. It provides food and shelter. It gives children the courage to feel good about themselves. The functioning family generates good feelings for everyone in the home.

Not every adult-child group is a family, just as not every house on the street is a real home. Families that don't work, that are diseased, are dysfunctional. Listen to what these teens say. If you or someone in your home does any of the following, you live in a dysfunctional family:

3

Alcohol abuse: (Alice, nineteen, graduated from high school last year and, as she says, got on the first bus out of town.) "I see now that my family was missing what I needed most: stability, support, love. Alcohol dissolved what love could have been there. When I was growing up as a part of it, I wasn't aware of that. All I felt was angry that my parents were not acting like parents. They were acting more like children with all their fighting and covering up the truth. I felt ashamed that my family lived under a storm cloud and that deep down we were different from normal families.

"Promises were made but not fulfilled. I'd get my head chewed off one day over nothing, and the next day I could have disappeared and no one would have noticed or cared.

"I wished I *could* disappear. I felt so alone even though I had sisters there with me. I thought no one else had ever felt the pain and loneliness I felt. It was as if we were all in this sinking ship; it was every man for himself. No one reached out to help the other; because our own needs were not being met, we had no capability of helping anyone else.

"I could never have friends over because I never knew when a fight would break out. Dad was like a volcano ready to blow at any moment. He was very unpredictable. I guess it doesn't matter much anyway because I can't remember having any friends that I would have had over. I guess because a friend is someone you can trust, and I had learned not to trust anyone.

"The cover-up in our house always seemed to have a good reason, like we'd blame it on 'this town.' People in 'this town' are so nosy they just want to know your business, they don't really care. They are all gossips, so we should not give out any information on the family. It was all such a lie and cover-up, but we all played along."

Drug abuse: (Barry is a sophomore. He is the only child in what most people would consider a well-to-do family.) "The message I get at home is—don't feel. Emotions are ugly and should be avoided. Ever since I was a kid Mom was going to the doctor for this or that, and at first I thought she was really sick. Then I realized that she takes prescription drugs for nonmedical reasons. Any time Mom begins to feel something, be it anger, disappointment, fear, or whatever, she takes something for it. She had a great system for keeping up her stock of 'medication.' She went to three or four doctors and they all gave her pills. That way she was never at a loss for something to take.

"Last night Mom and Dad argued—a real shouting match—and then Dad left. Next morning Mom acted as if nothing had happened. My stomach hurts but I pretend right along with her, and sometimes I take a couple of her Valiums to calm myself down and stop feeling so many emotions. They hurt. It's so nice just to be numb and feel nothing at all."

Physical abuse: (Roberto is in junior high. He's the oldest of a large family.) "You walk on eggshells at my house. One false move and you're in deep trouble. My friends at school joke about how their old man clobbers them and slaps them around. I don't laugh. When I was ten my father threw me against a wall so hard it broke the plaster, not to mention two ribs and my collarbone. I have missed school many times because of bruises I was afraid the teacher might notice and ask about. You ask why do I put up with it? Why don't I just slug him back? Why don't I run away? Right, man! Like where am I supposed to go? I don't have any money. And anyway if I leave he'll take it out on my sisters and little brother, and they have enough problems growing up in such a crazy house. And Momma, well, she already takes a lot of punches that were intended for me, so I can't go to her for help. All she can do is say a prayer for me. I just need to try harder to please him. These things are my own fault. Momma says it's just his way of showing that he loves us."

Sexual abuse: (Tomika is now twelve years old. She is in court-ordered therapy after the arrest and conviction of her father.) "I felt really special when Daddy would take me for long drives in the country. He would park the car and hold me close. It felt strange when he first touched me between the legs, but he said it was his special way of showing he loved me. I loved my Daddy and wanted him to love me, so I did whatever he liked.

"I was confused. As the months went by I didn't want to go for rides with Daddy anymore. Mom said I had to go so 'Daddy would be happy.' I wonder if she knew what was going on. I know my sister was jealous of the special attention Daddy gave me. I can't tell them why, or they'd call me a liar.

"Daddy kept telling me it was okay to show love this way, but then he would say it was our little secret and to tell no one. I tried to stop him. I said I was going to tell my teachers. He blew up. He said if I told anyone he and Mom would have to get a divorce and it would be all my fault. I never told.

"I have to do what he wants. If I didn't love him so much none of this would have happened—its all my fault."

Neglect of emotional needs: (Victoria is a high school senior in a nice small town. By all outward appearances she is happy and a high achiever. She volunteers for everything and always gets involved in activities to keep busy. Some might call her a workaholic.) "From the outside we appeared to have a perfect little family and a perfect little house. Well, the house wasn't so little. My brother and I each had our own bedroom and bathroom, which was great because we needed a place to hide.

"What we valued most was looking good. We had all the most fashionable clothes and took vacations in all the right places. I went to Paris for my summer vacation. But no matter what cool clothes we wore or cool places we went, we were still unhappy inside.

"As Dad got more and more successful we saw him less and less. He would come home late for dinner, talk about the news he had heard on the car radio, then be off to some committee meeting or cocktail party. Mom always seemed to be busy with her charity work and her clubs. I looked great on the outside, but I was a mess inside. Nobody in our house talked about what was really going on between people. In our house everything was always 'fine,' no one raised his voice. I kept everything inside and didn't rock the boat. But I wanted to do something special that would get my father's and mother's attention, so I tried out for the lead in the school play. Wow—I was thrilled when I got the part! I didn't think I had a chance because—well, the other kids are better at schoolwork and more popular than I am. But when I got the part I decided to give it all I had! I was the first to have all my lines learned, and I came early and stayed late at rehearsals. Nobody realized what a great escape this was from home. And after all, I did have a lot of experience 'acting.'

"But on opening night my family did not come to see me. They had other very important things to do. My mother did come by herself the second night and later said I did a good job. The show ran for three nights. We got rave reviews and had standing room only on the last night. We were a big hit! But my father and brother never saw all the work I did. The other kids' families came backstage after the show to kiss and hug them and shower them with flowers and praise. I always disappeared into the bathroom when this happened because it made me feel so sad and empty inside. I got recognition from the director and honors at the annual drama club banquet for 'Best Actress in the Creation of a Character,' and some of my fellow actors were kind enough to praise me, but I never reached the people I wanted to reach the most—my family."

If any of these stories is reflected in your home, you live in a dysfunctional family. In later chapters we'll see how Tomika and Roberto and the others tried to cope with their families, sometimes tragically, sometimes successfully.

When one member of the family breaks, the whole system begins to fall in on itself. Because the parents don't act like adults, you may have to act as a mother to your mom or a big brother to your dad. You're trapped and robbed, because this is the time in your life when you need true adult guidance and support more than ever. You are the kid, and they are robbing you of your childhood.

In your family everyone suffers and everyone needs help. You don't want your friends to see the ugliness in your home. You are isolated. The truth becomes hidden so deep that everyone in the house seems to forget what the real problem is. One alcoholic's son said it was as if an elephant were sitting in the middle of the living room and everyone just ignored it. No matter whom the disease starts with—mother, father, aunt, uncle, older brother— like a cancer it spreads and affects everyone it touches. The whole family lies, pretending the problem is not there. Trust is shattered, everyone is in pain, and the pain lasts for years. All the bad things you've learned need to be unlearned and replaced with more sane and peaceful ways of living in a family.

This is not a "blaming" book. It is not written to give you a finger to point at Mom or Dad or Uncle Fred and say, "That's why I have problems!" This is a survival manual for teens caught in dysfunctional families. It will give you a chance to see how others have been caught and how they broke loose. We do not intend this to be a "preaching manual" either; we are aware that religion is sometimes helpful, but it cannot always help us decide what to do about our situation. Saying a prayer may help us through the rough spots, but we are seeking ways of release from the victim role that dysfunctional families force us into.

This is a book about truth. It gives you a chance to face the truth of your life and how it is affecting you. If yours is a dysfunctional family the truth is that you are caught in what seems like a hopeless situation. Fear, anger, and despair are common emotions. Anyone caught in this kind of pain dreams of escape, and it is essential to detach yourself from the dysfunctional family if you are to survive. Sometimes the dreams turn into hollow fantasies or, worse, night- mares. Teens who thought they were getting out only got caught in another trap. By hearing their stories you can avoid the mistakes of turning to drugs, or constantly giving love and never getting any in return, or not being able to stand the pain any more and committing suicide.

You can run, but you can't hide. You need some one adult to let you know that you make a difference, you are important, you matter, and you should not be lost to the world. *You are a valuable human being.*

As members of dysfunctional families we have some things in common. We all experience to some degree one or all of the following emotions:

- **Distrust.** We have a need for control, and we dis- trust because our own developmental years were

spent in such volatile and unpredictable circumstances. We rely on no one but ourselves, but we would like to learn to be more open to others. Denial and cover-up are what we're used to. We would like to learn to let go and give someone all the responsibilities we carry on our shoulders.
- **Low self-esteem.** We are too self-critical, always blaming and finding fault with ourselves. We feel lots of guilt.
- **Inability to have fun.** We are so full of anger, disgust, depression, and sadness that we take ourselves too seriously and find it hard to laugh at our mistakes.

As a member of a dysfunctional family you know that the other members of the family cannot provide for you as they should. So you need to learn skills for finding a successful way out. Escape—but not to something worse. Make your life better than it would be if you let things continue as they are. You cannot control your family, but you can dream and plan a better life for yourself and the family that you may create in the future. You will want to give your children all the love and attention and care-filled parenting that you were deprived of.

You have already taken a step in that direction by choosing to read this book. Read and talk and seek help. You are not alone. You are suffering the loss of innocence; you have had to become your own parent, and parenting is the most difficult job in the world. Don't be too hard on yourself. You've been through a lot—things can only get better from here!

CHAPTER 2

Alcohol Abuse and the Broken Family

A lice was nineteen years old, just at that crucial point between teenager and adult, but her eyes seemed older. "I feel as though I am a refugee from a war," she told us. Her father was—is—an untreated alcoholic, so in a way Alice *was* caught in a war, a day-to-day battle in her own home. This is her story.

I grew up in a little town in Michigan. My parents were both from big cities and wanted their kids to grow up in the quiet of the countryside.

I remember Dad took me ice fishing once. I must have been about nine or ten years old. We walked out to a cold, dark shanty set up in the middle of the frozen lake. I was very scared; if the ice broke I couldn't swim and neither could he, and it was so dark and cold. But I was determined not to show my fear.

We stood there for what seemed like hours with our fish lines in the hole through the ice. Dad drank from the vodka bottle that he had brought along to keep himself warm, but I just stood in silence, my nose, fingers, and toes burning cold. At first I tried to make conversation, telling about something that happened at school, but Dad told me to be quiet because I was scaring away the fish.

Finally we gave up and trudged back to the car. I was hungry but I had to wait because he wouldn't let me come into the bar where he stopped. There I sat in the parking lot of a bar at nearly midnight. I was cold and hungry and now lonely. I was beginning to feel angry too. But I didn't show it. Never show it. What good would it do? Just start an argument.

It's funny how a ten-year-old can tell that Dad drinks too much but her thirty-five-year-old mother can't—or won't. I've read that all alcoholics have an "enabler," someone who lets the alcoholic drink too much. Mom allowed him to continue with his behavior even though she hated it. She still hesitates to label him an alcoholic, even after all this time and the ugly divorce proceedings.

My family was definitely sick. But I kept saying to myself that every family has some kind of problem to overcome, and that he was ours. So we continued the day-to-day problems of living with an alcoholic. Let me clarify that he drank every single day like this, not just once in a while: *every day.*

I had an older sister and a younger brother. "Had" is a good word: They're gone now, no more brother and sister than if they were two strangers I met on the street. Our family consisted of five people trying to hide from each other, all pretending that there was no problem at all. Mom would avoid Dad's angry drunken tirades and still put on a picture of the perfect family. My sister stayed at home—there were weeks during the summer when I don't think she left her room for more than an hour a day. My brother hid from everyone including himself, turning inward to his fantasy world of science fiction until he lost contact with the real world entirely.

Here's how a typical evening went: After school my brother would slouch in a chair reading one of his *Conan the Barbarian*-type stories. He was smart in a book-way but weird around the edges, my friends would say. My sister would watch game shows or cartoons, oblivious of the rest of the world. No friends, no interests besides the TV. Mom would be busy making dinner. The house was always neat and tidy.

We would eat dinner at six o'clock. Of course, Dad wasn't home, even though he got out of work at four-thirty. There was a choice of three taverns on the way home where he could "relax." Sometimes he would hit all three.

After dinner, while we did the dishes, Mom would make a plate for him, cover it with aluminum foil, and leave it in the oven. When the last dish was dried and put away we kids disappeared into our rooms. Mom sat in the living room reading her *Good Housekeeping* magazine. When we heard Dad's car pull into the driveway we would close our bedroom doors.

Almost every night there would be an argument. It would be over things like the leftover dinner was too dried out or too hot or cold. Dad didn't make too much sense when he was drunk, but Mom would jump right in trying to defend herself by yelling back at him.

The cursing and threats would get louder and

angrier. I knew he kept a gun in the house, supposedly to protect us against burglars, but I was terrified that he would kill my mother or himself or all of us. He would rave on like a maniac and doors would slam and Mom would sleep on the couch as she has for years. Sometimes if he was really ugly she would call the police, and a squad car would come to our house. I could hear my father saying, "I never laid a hand on her," and then the police would try to calm them both down.

The next day Mom would act as if nothing had happened.

I can't blame it all on her. We all acted as if nothing had happened, that night or any night. What else could we do? We had to get on with school and homework and stuff, so we just tried to ignore it.

The threats didn't stop with Mom. As much as we tried, we couldn't spend all our time shut in our rooms. There were weekends and holidays. How I hate holidays, especially Christmas. Everything about Christmas seems to emphasize families, and mine was just too much. Christmas just gave Dad an excuse to drink more.

Vacations were another exercise in tolerance. We would drive until we came to a bar where Dad would stop for a quick one. I remember the many vacations that Mom, my brother, sister, and I spent sitting in a hot car in a bar's parking lot. If Mom complained when Dad got back in the car, he would drive like a maniac, speeding up and zooming past cars until Mom shut up. We three kids would clutch the back seat, terrified. I guess we were just lucky we weren't killed in a wreck on one of our so-called vacations.

I confronted Dad once. I was in eighth grade and

wanted to go to a friend's house or something like that. He was supposed to drive me, but he never showed up. When he finally did get home I told him I was mad and disappointed. He started to yell at me as he always did to Mom, but I wouldn't let him have any excuses. I told him that he had promised to give me a ride and that I was angry that he didn't show up. He started to make excuses. I said I didn't believe his sob story. Suddenly he turned and slapped me right across the face. I stood there a second, frozen. He had never hit me before. Stunned but even more defiant, I said, "Go ahead and hit me, beat me 'til I'm black and blue, but you'll never change how much I hate you!" He staggered backwards. His eyes were blood-shot, but I could tell I had hurt him—and that made me feel good.

He grabbed the six-pack he had brought home from the tavern and stormed out. The tires squealed as he roared out of the driveway. I remember wishing he would crash into a tree and die.

My mother tried to comfort me, but I was too angry to listen to her. I needed to be alone to think, so I headed for my room. My brother and sister stood in their bedroom doorways through the whole thing but didn't say a word. I walked to my room, closed the door, and vowed to myself that I would get out of that house.

Mom said that we should keep it to ourselves. Not in so many words, of course. It was the neighbors' fault (in our family it was always somebody else's fault) that we had to keep to ourselves. They were too nosy. "These people only want to know your business," she would say to us as far back as I can remember.

As I grew older I would use any excuse not to be

around in the evenings when Dad got home. I wasn't old enough to drive, so I hung around with kids who could. After school we would pile into someone's car and go to a friend's house or hang out at the mall.

One friend was Renee. Her family had their own business, her brother was in college, and her mom worked for a lawyer. In the afternoon we would go to Renee's house.

Renee seemed rich to me. Her dad gave her a new car for her sixteenth birthday, and she always wore fashions right out of *Seventeen* magazine. We would go to her house because she had the newest albums and videos. She also drank.

Lots of kids did in high school. "I need a drink to unwind," she'd tell us and help herself from her dad's liquor cabinet. We drank cherry vodka, Coke and rum, and gin and 7-Up. Sometimes four or five of us girls would be there after school, especially on Friday night before the dance. Renee said her parents didn't mind if she drank at home. They told her it was better for a teenager to drink at home than shoot drugs in an alley.

Renee was hilarious after a few drinks. She'd tell the most outrageous stories, and we would laugh 'til tears rolled down our cheeks. This was a lot better than being around Dad. A couple of rum and Cokes made the world seem a little happier to me, too.

The last time I went to Renee's house was a Saturday afternoon. Her parents were away, and a full-blown party was going on. Kids from her brother's college and from our high school were there. Everyone was drinking. I had to leave early, and I'm glad I did. More and more kids kept coming, and the street was packed with cars. Windows were broken and a big fight broke out. The neighbors called the police, who broke up the party. I heard later that her parents found Renee passed out in the bathroom when they finally got home.

I don't know what Renee's parents did to her. She wasn't in school the rest of the year.

Renee's drinking was no better than my father's, even though Renee became funnier the more she drank. She couldn't control it. Maybe I was going to be like that too. I just had to control it. I had to control my life more if I was going to make it.

I joined clubs at school. Mom never complained when I said I had to stay after school to work on the yearbook or practice my speech for debate club. At one time I was in five different after-school groups.

Being with other kids outside of school, I began to see how weird my family was. I never invited anyone to my house, but I would go to other kids' houses to rehearse our parts in the school play, and sometimes I would stay for dinner. What a difference! The whole family would eat at the same time and actually talk to each other.

The more I saw of the real world, the more I realized I had to get away from the sickness that had eaten away the soul of our home. But I didn't want to just run away from my family; I wanted to run *to* something better.

I had to get away from my family before I was swallowed up in the nightmare. My parents' marriage consisted of an endless series of no-win fights. Dad was a failure and took his faults out on us. Mom let him abuse her, let him abuse us, let him abuse himself. She didn't care about anything except keeping up appearances for the neighbors. She had failed too but wouldn't—or couldn't—admit it. I think if she had told Dad to quit drinking and *really meant it*, instead of just nagging and whining at him, he might have tried to stop. Like a commercial I saw on TV where a wrecking ball smashes into a nice cozy house, breaking through the walls, knocking over the furniture, and smashing the family picture on the fireplace mantel, Dad's drinking had destroyed our whole home and everything in it.

The one thing I learned from Renee was that money could give you freedom. She had used her freedom to get drunk; I wanted to use mine to divorce myself from the family that was dragging me down.

I got a job as a waitress because that was the easiest job to get when you were only fifteen years old. I worked after school and on weekends. I got two rewards for working: I escaped from the house, and I made money. Every night I walked out of work with tips in my pocket, which I used for spending money. Every two weeks when I got my regular paycheck I put it into a savings account in the bank.

Because my job took up my after-school time, I dropped out of most of my clubs, but I stuck with journalism club. My boss let me schedule work around club meetings. I wanted to be in this club because our advisor, Mr. Adams, was so cool. I don't mean just good-looking either. He talked to you like another adult who knew what was going on. He told us about his time in college, and I decided I was going to go to college too. I was no A student in school. Good grades were never easy for me, especially in math and science, but I found that if I tried I could get good enough grades to make it through. Extra studying gave me another excuse not to be around my family. I began to learn that you are only out of luck when you give up.

No one else in my family had gone to college. My older sister got a job in a factory after she graduated from high school. She still lives at home, and I doubt if she talks to anyone at work. I never wanted to end up there. I didn't want to be a waitress the rest of my life either.

I didn't talk to anyone at home about my decision to go to college. Mom would have said, "Oh, that's nice to have a dream, dear, but we can't afford it." My sister would have been jealous and argued that no one could go to college because she hadn't gone. And my little brother wasn't someone I could share with. We had played together when we were little kids, but he had been under our family too long.

No way was I going to talk to Dad.

Getting into college was the hardest thing I had ever done. I applied to a big university that was three hours away. I thought about applying to an out-of-state college, but it cost too much. I checked into ways of paying for college and found that I could get a scholarship and a loan for my tuition and be in a work-study program to pay my living expenses. My counselor and Mr. Adams helped a lot by getting information for me on how and where to apply.

By the time I needed Mom to cosign my loan, I had already been accepted at the university and gotten my scholarship. There was no way she could say no. I was on my way.

Last September I left "home." School is hard, but I am free. I am going to live my own life.

I said that getting into college was the hardest thing I had ever done. As I look back now, the paperwork of getting accepted and getting financial aid was difficult, but the hardest thing I did was to make the decision to go to college. That decision was my declaration of independence. I couldn't live with my family anymore. It would have been an easy thing to do though. The easy way out would have been just to stay where I was. Mom was a great enabler. She not only enabled my father to drink, she set up situations that enabled my sister not to get along with anyone. "They're not good enough for you," she'd say. She enabled my little brother to stay tied to her apron strings, treating him like a fragile baby, enabling him to retreat into his fantasy world day after day.

I guess I still carry the scars of my childhood. I read in psychology class that children of alcoholics have problems years later. Perhaps I will never be free of all the ugly memories, but at least for now I have established my way of dealing with the pressures.

Some people might criticize me, saying that I've run away from my family's problems rather than face them. But I haven't run away—I'm running *to* a whole new world with people who are more calm and understanding. I am my own mother and father, sister and brother. Now I can grow and change and plan a happier future for myself. I have the freedom to laugh and cry and feel all those emotions that have been bottled up inside me for so many years. I used to say to myself, "He is just trying to make me cry," but I refused to cry. I would never let him see me cry.

Now I am strong. The game is over. I have won.

Alice was able to cope with her dysfunctional family by divorcing herself from their sickness. Rather than turning her frustration and anger inward against her own self-esteem—which many children of dysfunctional families do—Alice turned that anger against the pain around her. Instead of being destructive, the anger become constructive. It gave her strength to break away and become her own person.

Alice, the daughter of an alcoholic, toyed with drinking herself. She found acceptance from the in-crowd at school through drinking. You may think it inconsistent that she would drink when alcohol was causing the problems in her home. However, alcoholism is a disease that is passed from generation to generation. If one of your parents drinks, your chances of becoming an alcoholic increase by 50 percent. If both your parents are alcohol abusers, your chances of becoming an alcoholic rise to 80 percent.

If you live in a dysfunctional family where the parents drink, you need help, you deserve help to get out. If you have started to drink yourself, you need to get that help as fast as you can. There are organizations that can help you keep from falling into the pit your parents are in. Several are listed in the Appendix. Contact them. If one group doesn't help, try another.

The old saying, "If at first you don't succeed, try again," is true when it comes to pulling yourself out of a dysfunctional family. You have been taught by your family's example to fail. The message they send is that something is wrong with you. You need to see the good in you and then act to let that good grow.

CHAPTER ◇ 3

Drug Abuse:

Numbing the Home

Sometimes when we think of drug abuse we imagine unshaven cocaine addicts using dirty needles in abandoned, burned-out crack houses. The real problem of drug abuse cuts across society and involves everyone from bank presidents and star athletes to high school students to unborn babies.

The devastation of drug use is that the personality of the user is destroyed. Our body naturally produces chemicals (drugs) that are used in every process from digesting food to thinking. These *natural* drugs can be "uppers" such as epinephrine (also known as adrenalin) that stimulate the nervous system, making your heart beat faster, the pupils of your eyes contract, and your muscles respond quickly. Or they can be natural painkillers known as endorphins that enable your body to tolerate pain. Some people who really push their bodies to the limit, like marathon runners, describe this natural release of endorphins as a euphoric "high."

Some forms of mental illness such as chronic depression are caused by malfunctions in the body's ability to produce and use its drug system. The effect of imbalances of chemicals in the brain is changes in personality.

When a person uses artificial drugs that enter the nervous system, a new person appears in the body of the one you knew. Every response he or she makes, from solving a problem to reacting with an emotion, is now influenced and distorted by that drug.

The terrible effect of drugs on the streets of America is reported every day on the evening news. The true terror of drugs is how they destroy our families.

Barry grew up in a "clean" middle-class family, not where you'd expect to find heavy drug use. But Barry's mother became addicted to prescription painkillers, and drug abuse destroyed their family before Barry could cry out for help.

The message in our house was clear: Don't feel. No matter how much anger or hurt was around, ignore it and it will go away.

Mom's headaches ruled our lives. Saturday mornings we tiptoed around the house because of her "migraines." Everything was hushed, the lights were out, the blinds closed. I remember the visiting nurses coming to the house, all dressed in white and smelling of antiseptic, to give Mom her Demerol shots for those headaches.

Her headaches got worse and worse. She went to three or four doctors at a time. Each gave her different prescriptions. In her bedroom drawer were shoeboxes filled with pill bottles.

If we made too much noise Mom would come out of her room screaming, her face red and contorted.

My sister Jill and I immediately became silent and cowered, trying to make ourselves small. Mom would throw our toys into a pile and jam them into the closet, threatening to throw them into the trash if we didn't shut up. She would pick on Jill because she was older, screaming at her until tears ran down Jill's face. Ten minutes later Mom would come back out of her room, hug and kiss us, give us cookies and milk, and say she didn't really mean to scare us. We would kiss her and hug her and everything would be nice—until the next blow-up.

Mom and Dad never argued. Maybe that's why they divorced. Dad's a salesman for a lumber supply company and travels a lot. Sometimes we didn't see him for three or four days. Usually he'd be home on weekends, then on Sunday night have to catch a late flight to be ready for his calls first thing Monday morning.

During football and basketball seasons he would take clients to the games on Saturdays. During the summer he would go on golf outings with his boss or other sales reps. When they met at our house we were shown off as the perfect family. Mom and Dad, son and daughter all smiling, a little showcase family on display.

Dad's world of sales required that he not show his feelings, that he project an image of an efficient, friendly, carefree man. That was the image I grew up with. Dad appeared as a background figure in our lives—someone who bought our big house, visited, but always lived in his own world, never approachable or understanding of our problems. Always stylishly dressed, with never a hair out of place, no one could measure up to his perfection.

Jill couldn't. I look at pictures of her, photos Mom keeps in boxes at the back of her closet, and I see a pretty, brown-eyed brunette, her long hair cascading over her shoulders. In all the pictures she's smiling, but that might just be because we always smile for the camera.

Jill couldn't live up to Mom's image of perfection. Things were always Jill's fault. It was Jill's responsibility to look after the house when Mom had her headaches. She made the dinners, folded laundry, cleaned the house, and never did things correctly enough for Mom.

After Mom was over one of her increasingly frequent headache spells she would review what Jill had done. "We don't fold the dish towels like this," she would say sarcastically. We never knew what to expect at dinner time. Mom would sit bleary-eyed at the table. If we were lucky she would eat in silence, take another pill, and go back to her room or lie on the living room sofa with a cold cloth over her eyes. However, something would usually tick her off. She would criticize the meat, complain about the vegetables, her voice icy and sharp, keeping it up until tears welled in Jill's eyes.

I felt sorry for Jill, but glad that it wasn't me, guilty that I didn't say anything to defend her, angry that Mom would be so judgmental. So many feelings would well up in me at one time that I ended up saying and doing nothing, staring at my plate until the storm blew over. After one of these assaults Mom would continue eating as if we had only been discussing the weather.

If this scene took place on one of those rare evenings when Dad ate at home, he would pretend that nothing out of the ordinary was happening, or worse yet, join in the attack on Jill.

Mom and Dad used "you" messages when they found fault: "*You* didn't make dinner right. *You* never listen to me. *You* dress like a slob. *You* are never going to amount to anything." These messages blamed Jill and me for what we are. They attacked us at our selves, always jabbing at us, pushing poisoning thoughts under our skins. Maybe we *were* slobs, maybe we never *would* have any value, maybe we *were* no good.

I see now that my parents were turning those messages into attacks on our very existence, on our self-esteem, on our own worth rather than an attack on the way we prepared the food. What they were saying was that *they* didn't like the things I did. *They* thought the way I dressed wasn't up to *their* standards of neatness. Or *they* were concerned about how well I was doing with my plans for the future. They hid their true intent, and feelings, behind hurtful words. How much more open and happy our lives would have been if they had used "I" instead of "you." When someone says, "*I* worry that you don't have sound plans for your future," it can open a conversation because it shows concern. If kids often hear "*You* will never amount to anything!" they start to believe it and give up on themselves, give up on life.

I hid from those stinging words and from not knowing when Mom would blow up at us and when she would be a walking zombie from her pills. I hid in food. Food gave me more than nutrition; it gave me pleasure and comfort. I felt emptiness on the inside, and maybe that's why I kept stuffing myself with junk food. I never had close friends when I was little. You need to share with friends, and I wasn't able to share my true feelings even with myself. Coke, candy, cookies, and cake were my friends. I got fat. I wasn't a jolly fat person though. I tore up a picture of myself in fourth grade because I couldn't stand the sight of my chubby cheeks. When we went to buy clothes I had to get jeans sized "chunky." Mom would tease me about how plump I was, but of course she kept stocking up on junk food.

Food became my addiction. Whenever I felt bad, I ate. I thought about food all the time. As soon as I got out of school I began to plan what I would have for a snack when I got home. I ate cupcakes, ice cream, anything sweet and filling. I ate peanut butter sandwiches with peanut butter half an inch thick and jelly globbed on so that it squished out between the slices of bread. I always had seconds at dinner, especially mashed potatoes and gravy.

Because of my weight I couldn't run or play as well as the other guys in my class. I was always the last one picked when teams were divided up. Gym class became a nightmare.

When I started junior high I felt lost. The message at home was *Don't feel, hide your feelings.* But now I felt hurt and alone. No one cared about me, I wasn't good at anything. The ache in my stomach was so bad that even food could not soothe it. To cover my insecurity and emptiness I began to pretend I was sure of myself. I became a "know-it-all," unruffled by anything. I would brag about what a big house we lived in, how cool it was that my sister Jill was in college. I would exaggerate how much money Dad made and boast about our great vacations, stretching the truth to make me sound better than anyone else.

I became a pretend self, a cardboard figure of who I really was. Hard, cold, stuck-up, better than anyone on the outside—all the while nervous, empty, false, and powerless on the inside. I couldn't grow because I was trapped inside the monster I had created. I didn't know where I was going or how I was going to get there.

One of Mom's many doctors had switched her off pain pills onto tranquilizers. She said he had told her that her headaches were due to stress. There was a lot of stress in our lives. Mom and Dad had begun to argue. If the argument got real bad Dad would slam out of the house and Mom would go in the bathroom and take pills. She would disappear into her room and sleep. I would lock up the house at bedtime, but leave the chain off the front door hoping that Dad would be back before morning.

One day I got in trouble at school because I told a teacher he was full of b.s. He had backed me into a corner because I was talking. He called on me and tried to embarrass me. "Maybe if you already know everything," he said, "you should get up in front and teach the class." Some of the kids started to giggle. I stood up and said I would probably do a better job because he was full of b.s. Everyone in class broke out laughing, and he kicked me out of class. The principal called my mother and then suspended me for the rest of the day. Mom thought it was probably the teacher's fault.

I knew I was wrong, but I had become so accustomed to hiding behind sarcasm and flippancy that it had become my first line of defense. With a kid like me, no wonder my parents were getting a divorce.

Mom was easier to get along with when she was

taking tranqilizers. She persuaded one of her doctors to prescribe another brand, so she was taking two different pills every day. Because she went to so many doctors, they didn't know how many kinds of pills she took. She also had prescriptions filled at several drugstores so the pharmacists wouldn't become suspicious. I guess all this hiding proves that she knew what she was doing was wrong, but she kept on doing it. Had she become a weak person, or had the pills screwed up her thinking?

She didn't argue anymore, she didn't yell anymore. She went around all day calm and quiet. Her headaches did go away, or at least she never complained about them anymore. Sometimes she acted a little drunk, not falling down or anything, just staggering a little or sitting and staring off into space.

Things were going okay until the beginning of December. Jill came home from college and announced that she was sure she had flunked all her classes. She said she wasn't good enough for college and had dropped out. Putting on a bright face, she said she had gotten a job at the mall. She worked there less than a week and then quit. She said it didn't pay well enough and that she'd get another job. She never did.

Jill pored over the want ads each night circling jobs and went out the next day all dressed up, but I don't think she ever really applied for jobs. She complained of being tired and began to spend a lot of time in her room, going to bed early, not even staying up to watch her favorite TV shows.

The week before Christmas she suddenly became brighter, more like her old self again. She called me into her room on Saturday. "Barry," she said, "you've always liked my stereo. I want you to have it because I know you'll take care of it, won't you?" Of course I would. It was a great stereo. Why she was giving it away I didn't know, but I wasn't about to argue with her. I found out later that she had given away other things to her friends, almost as if she were putting up her most prized possessions for adoption.

She kissed everyone goodnight that evening. The next morning she was dead.

I couldn't believe it, my own sister committing suicide. My mother found her in bed in the morning and began screaming and screaming. Dad called 911. Our house filled with police, and a second ambulance came and took my mother to the hospital. I sat in the living room waiting for Dad to get back from the hospital, completely numb except for the burning gnawing in my stomach.

I went into the kitchen and ate half of a jelly doughnut, but it made me sick. I ran into the bathroom to throw up. My hands shook uncontrollably, the room spun. I needed to calm down. Everything would be okay if I could get control of myself.

I opened the bathroom medicine cabinet and saw Mom's pills. Maybe one of those would help me too. I took two, but I didn't feel any better. I took two more and two of her leftover pain pills just to stop the hurt. I went back downstairs, taking the bottle with me. I began to feel a little calmer. I sat on the sofa and ate the pills one by one. I just wanted to feel better.

I woke up in the emergency room flat on my back with a big tube down my throat gagging me, my arms tied down while the doctors pumped my stomach. I spent Christmas, and the next three months, in a mental hospital.

Pine View, that's the name of the hospital, isn't like the nuthouses you see in the movies with chains and bars. It's more like a big hotel or dormitory. I shared a room with another guy my age, and we had pool tables and TVs in the rec room and could wear normal clothes, not hospital pajamas. It isn't like a prison either. The doctors and nurses don't dress in white; they dress like regular people, some in blue jeans even. Slowly I learned to trust them, to let them see the empty hurt I felt inside. We did a lot of "group work," all the guys sitting in a circle with one of the nurses directing the conversation. These groups helped me see that I wasn't so different from others and that what I did with my life depended on my own decisions, not just the decisions my parents made.

At first I just pretended to share my feelings, still covering up the loneliness I felt. But then I began to feel that these people really did care about me, really wanted to help. One nurse, Maggie, helped a lot by listening to me talk about how I was brought up, how I felt as if I was all alone even when I was in a crowd. In one of our private talks I confessed to her how small and ashamed I felt, no matter how I boasted.

Sometimes I cried like a baby talking to her, remembering how alone I had been while growing up. She said it was okay to cry. It helped to release the pent-up feelings of loss that I didn't even know I had. It's important to let the trapped feelings out. But developing self-esteem, a love of yourself, is the cornerstone of recovering your life. To value yourself, you have to know who you are. We spent weeks, both in group time and private sessions, doing values clarification so that I could start to see who I really am and to learn to like and respect that true me.

I learned that my mother's dependency on pills destroyed her ability to give her children the most critical thing in life, a positive feeling about ourselves. I began to accept that her drug abuse was not my fault and to see that the future could be different from the dark past.

I left the hospital last spring. I still see a psychologist once a month, and Mom and I go to a family therapist every week to keep trying to repair the damage of the past. While I was in Pine View, Mom went through a detoxification program to get off drugs.

Our family broke down so badly that it destroyed an irreplaceable part of itself. We're doing our best to get what's left to work. None of it is easy, but it's a price we are all willing to pay for what happened to Jill. Nothing will ever bring her back, but we owe it to her to try harder in her memory.

Barry's dysfunctional family had to be destroyed before he or his parents could begin to rebuild it. Often the drug-induced ways of thinking and feeling are so all-encompassing that the individual must hit rock bottom before being able to see what the problem is. Sometimes, as it was for Jill, it is too late.

Teenage suicide is a problem in modern American society. Nearly 7,000 teens kill themselves each year, and that number is only the confirmed deaths by suicide. Police suspect that many accidents such as drownings and automobile fatalities may be intentional.

Suicide is a crying out for help, a desperate cry that life itself has become too painful to bear. Warning signs of suicide are the following: (1) A sudden improvement in the mood of a person who has been depressed. This may mean that the person is relieved at having have made up his mind to do it. (2) A person tells you that he or she is going to kill himself and has a specific plan worked out to do it. *Take that seriously.* (3) A depressed person begins to give away prized possessions for others to take care of. If you know someone showing any or all of these signs, or you recognize them in yourself, get professional help now. Phone numbers are listed in the Appendix. If you cannot reach one of those numbers, check the Yellow Pages phone directory under Crisis Intervention or call the operator.

Initially Barry tried to cope with the pain of a dysfunctional family by eating. It is not uncommon for children with an addicted parent to develop an addiction of their own. However, this way of coping only causes more problems, as it did for Barry's self-esteem. One of the problems Barry will need to continue to work on, with the help of his monthly sessions with his psychologist, is to build ways of handling stress other than eating. One of the worst things Barry could do is to follow a fad diet that tries to make you lose weight by eating weird foods or only one kind of food. People may lose weight on these diets, but research has shown that they gain the weight right back when they resume regular meals. The only kinds of diets that really work are those that change the way you eat, such as Weight Watchers, or weight-loss clinics under medical supervision. These methods not only tell you what kinds of food to eat, they also provide support from the others in the group.

Barry's weight, however, was just a symptom of his inability to cope. Just as a person with a broken leg would go to a hospital to have it set, people with emotional problems sometimes need to go to hospitals, too. As Barry found out, mental hospitals are not the loony bins sometimes shown in old movies. Modern hospitals are set up to treat mental and emotional illness just as regular hospitals treat physical ills.

Of course, if you can be treated in a doctor's office or a clinic it is better than being stuck in a hospital. If you feel that there is a need in your life for professional healing, ask your doctor for referral to a mental health worker. If you don't have a doctor, talk to your social worker or counselor at school. The school system has programs to help kids. If you belong to a church, ask the minister to recommend someone for you to talk with.

If none of these are people you can talk to, call your hospital and ask their referral service to give you names to call. Keep on trying! There is no reason you should suffer until a crisis forces the world to see how much pain is in your house. Don't wait until it's too late.

CHAPTER 4

Physical Abuse, Verbal Abuse, Mental Cruelty

S ome homes become battlefields. Invisible land mines are planted by the parents: restrictive rules, impossible goals, or unstated expectations. When a child steps on one of these by accident, his parents' wrath explodes into deadly violence.

Each year millions of children are abused by their parents. Think about that. The mother and father who are supposed to support and love their kids are beating them. If these parents slapped, kicked, or hit a stranger on the street they would be jailed for years as a menace to society. Yet their own children in their own home are regularly beaten because it's "good for them."

Perhaps the worst part of this cruelty is that it teaches children that it is okay for parents to hit. They grow up to become parents who hit their kids, and those kids will grow up to hit their kids too. A cycle of parents-hitting-children (for whatever reason) may be started by only one abusive adult. Child abuse then becomes a family legacy passed on generation to generation for a hundred years unless someone stops it.

When Roberto's father was a small boy growing up in Europe his father had never hesitated to use a leather belt to whip his children. Part of Roberto's father's "macho image" was that he had always been able to take those beatings "like a man," which meant, of course, never to cry. He also took the example of those beatings to heart and became a parent suffering from unseen scars of anger and distrust. This is how Roberto grew up...

My pop works hard to give us the things we've got. We have a nice apartment although it has only two bedrooms. My parents have one bedroom, my sisters share the other. My brothers and I sleep on the fold-out sofa bed in the living room. I am the oldest boy.

Momma works during the day doing laundry, cooking, and keeping the apartment neat. I have to make my bed and carry the trash out to the dumpster, but my sisters help her clean and cook. We try to keep everything spotless because my father is a very particular man. When he comes home we must have everything perfect. If one small thing is wrong he will yell at us, he will scream at our mother.

"You are a pig," he will shout. "I must work all day, and you cannot even keep a house!" I have seen him slap Momma's face, and she would cry and beg to be forgiven.

We were always spanked when we were little. Momma would spank us for not putting our toys away or for talking too loud. When we got older she would say, "Wait 'til your father gets home!" when we did something wrong. As soon as Pop got in the door she would list all the things we had done wrong. He'd scowl at us, pull off his belt, and push us into the back bedroom, where he would hit us on the butt, back, and thighs. After a beating from Pop you had to stand for hours because your bottom hurt so bad.

School was no piece of cake for me. My teachers told my parents that I was smart but didn't apply myself. That really made Pop mad. In fifth grade I got a D on my report card for handwriting. My teacher added the note, "Roberto needs to improve." I don't know what kind of family she thought I had. Did she think Momma and Pop would sit down with me at the kitchen table with cookies and milk and practice dotting Is and crossing Ts? I knew what was going to happen when Pop saw that D.

Walking home, I dreamed of running away but knew it was no use. I folded the report card and jammed it in my back pocket as I climbed the front stoop of our apartment building.

I didn't say it was report card day. Momma didn't mention anything about it. Neither did Pop when he got home. I went to bed that night sure that I had gotten away with it.

Suddenly at midnight Pop pulled me out of bed waving the report card in my face. He called me a criminal for hiding it. Why was I so bad? he yelled at me. Why was I trying to hide this? He began slapping my face. I tried to cover my head but he punched me so hard in the stomach that I fell to the floor. I couldn't breathe.

I must have passed out. I woke up in my bed in the morning. Momma gave us breakfast as if nothing had happened. It could have been a bad dream except for the bruises on my arm where Pop had grabbed me and my aching stomach. After that I didn't think of teachers as helping me.

As I got older I tried to stay out of the house. In the summer a bunch of guys who lived in the building hung out together. We played basketball and baseball in an empty lot. It was kind of a playground paved with cracked cement, with a broken swing set at one end and a basketball hoop at the other.

We could only play basketball when Carlos played, because it was his ball. One day we were waiting for him and began throwing pieces of broken cement at the backboard to see who would come closest to the center. The stones made a whacking, ringing sound when they hit the metal backboard. We kept throwing bigger and bigger chunks of cement to make louder gongs. I found a hunk the size of my fist. I reared back and tossed it with all my might. It missed the backboard and went sailing over the fence. In almost slow motion I watched it fall right down into the side window of a car parked on the street. Like it was a perfect shot, the rock hit the window. There was a scrapping pop and the window blew apart into a million pieces.

We stood frozen for a minute, then scattered.

"Hey, you!" yelled a man in a blue raincoat who was coming out of the store across the street. It must have been his car. I ran faster. Jules had to run straight past the guy to get home. He crouched down low and put on the speed, but the man caught him. I didn't look back. I climbed the fence, jumped down and ran around to the front of the building. I ran up the stairs as if the guy was right behind me, got to our door, and stopped. No one had followed me. I had made it safe!

I went in, turned on the TV, and pretended nothing had happened.

When Pop came home, Momma had no bad report to give him. I had been outside all day. He grunted, got a beer from the fridge, and sat in his easy chair to read the newspaper.

There was a heavy knock at the door, and Momma hurried to answer it. She talked for a minute and then called Pop over. I looked around the corner to see who it was, and froze. There was the man in the blue raincoat and the police.

Pop talked with them at the door. I could hear his tone of voice, but I couldn't catch everything he said. He was soothing them, turning on the charm. "Boys will be boys," I heard him say. He came back into the living room to get his wallet out of his jacket. As he walked by me he gave me a look that made me cringe.

He gave the man in the blue raincoat a lot of money. The policeman asked if that was enough; the man nodded, and they left. I sat in my corner of the sofa, the palms of my hands slippery with sweat, my mouth dry.

"Roberto," said Pop, his voice cold and hard, "go to the bedroom." I stood up slowly. "Now," he yelled, and I dashed down the hall. He threw me across the bed. "You good-for-nothing!" he cursed.

He pulled off his belt and began to hit me with it harder and harder.

"You're worthless! Worthless punk!" He hit me again and again, then threw the belt at me, swore, and slammed out of the room.

I didn't begin to cry until he left the room. I lay across the bed, my back stinging, alone in the dark.

No one came to help me. His words ran like a broken record in my head.

Once my brother Petey showed up at school with a black eye. He had dropped a dish at dinner the night before. Pop had yelled at him and shoved the side of his head against the wall to knock some sense into him.

Petey's teacher asked him how he got the black eye. Petey, the dummy, told her Pop did it. She told the principal, and he called Momma and Pop in for a conference.

Momma said Petey made it up, that he'd gotten the black eye when he tripped. He was a clumsy kid. Pop said of course he disciplined his kids, but that he never hurt them. Petey was at the conference too, but he just sat through the whole thing. He knew he had made a big mistake to blame Pop for his own clumsiness.

When they got home they locked Petey in the hall closet to teach him not to spread lies about the family.

By the time I got to high school the whole school thing was getting to be a bore. The teachers were stupid, and the classes were a real drag.

Mr. Owens, my wimpy English teacher, would let us have passes for sixth hour to study in the library. Me and the guys would cut the rest of the day. We'd hang around by the bridge behind school, smoking cigarettes and shooting the breeze. Carlos had a car and (when it was running) we'd cruise around town. He was older, and we'd buy a six-pack with his fake ID for some liquid refreshment in the afternoon.

Cops would drive by, and we'd duck down so they couldn't see us. Once at a stop light Carlos was sucking a brew when some cops pulled up next to him. He slammed the can down so fast it foamed all over his jeans. When the light changed and the cops pulled away I thought we would die laughing.

This was a whole lot more exciting than hanging around at home. I was fourteen years old. I didn't need to take any more crap from anybody.

We needed money to put gas in Carlos's car. Jimmy thought we should rob a bank. What a dumb dweeb! Then they told me I had to come up with the money or forget hanging around with them. Where was I going to get the money?

The next morning my brothers and sisters got ahead of me on the walk to school. I kept trying to think of where I was going to get the money to stay in the gang when I saw a little kid get off the city bus alone. He would have money for the bus trip home, maybe lunch money too.

No one was around, so I pointed down a side alley. "Hey kid, look at that," I said. He turned down the alley to see, and I pushed him up against the wall. His eyes got real big.

"Kid, why don't you lend me your lunch money," I said, grabbing his shirt.

Tears grew in his eyes. He fumbled in his pocket and gave me the buck and a half he had. His hand shook as he gave it to me. I warned him not to squeal on me or else. I told him he better give me tomorrow's money too. Then I punched him in the gut to let him know I meant business.

The guys thought I was great when I told them how I had strong-armed the kid. If you want it, you take it!

We tooled around in Carlos's car for a while. We saw an old lady pulling a small grocery cart. Her purse lay on top of her groceries. We pulled up next to her, and Jimmy jumped out and grabbed her purse. She screamed as he jumped back into the car. Carlos burned rubber. A man ran yelling out of the house across the street. He ran after us, but Carlos squealed around the corner and lost him.

We dug through the lady's purse and found five bucks. Everybody was laughing. I laughingly told Jimmy he should have knocked the old hag down to keep her from screaming. He said if I was such a tough guy I should do the next grab. We cruised around. There was an armored truck outside the bank. They said how about I grab that. I told them maybe tomorrow.

I needed to show these guys how tough I was. We saw an old man walking home from the bank. He looked like a retired old fart that had just cashed his Social Security check. Go for it, the guys said. They were all looking at me. I got out of the car.

"Hey, old man, loan me five bucks," I said. But he kept on walking, pretending not to hear me. "Hey, old man, I'm talking to you." I grabbed his sleeve. "Give me five bucks!"

"I'll give you five!" he snarled. Turning toward me, he swung his cane like a bat. He cracked me across the side of my face. The sharp pain in my eye froze me for a second. He kept hitting at me with the cane, yelling and swearing. I held tight to his arm. He hit me on the face, on my shoulders. He beat at me the way Pop did.

Something inside me ripped loose. Still holding his arm, I slugged him hard in the face. He stumbled back, blood on his mouth, his cane raised in front of him. I grabbed it. I hit him as hard as I could. I put everything I had into it. I hit him again and again and again. He fell down moaning. I broke the cane hitting him. I stepped on him as he tried to crawl away and began to kick him.

I remember Jimmy trying to pull me off. I heard the police sirens coming. No one was going to stop me. I had to punish this old man. I had to punish this old man for hitting me.

Roberto had tried to store all the anger and hurt his parents had poured on him. That is impossible for anybody. All his trapped feelings exploded at once. The only way he had learned to express his feelings was through violence.

The excitement of joining a gang, breaking the rules, appealed to Roberto because his ability to feel normal had literally been beaten out of him. One abused boy, when asked by a social worker to list all the different emotions, was amazed that there were so many: He thought there were only happiness and anger.

Anger, and avoiding it, controls the lives of victims of abuse. The whole house is filled with exploding anger, but the kids are taught by severe punishment not to express their own anger. Everyone else in the house blows up at the slightest incident, taking their anger out on the kids. The kids not only have to shelve their own angry feelings but also absorb the anger their parents dish up daily.

The human body is not made to bottle up large quantities of anger or other stress. Anger is like an acid. It will eat its way out of the bottle sooner or later, with terrible results.

One way the body deals with anger is to change it into another emotion. An angry kid may feel tremendous waves of guilt. That is natural. Everything the child sees growing up—TV, books, movies—tells him that he is supposed to love Mom and Dad. But these people hurt him. The very people who are to protect him in the world are the cruelest to him. The conflicting emotions of love and hate crash together to make guilt. This is turned inward, and the child feels that all the problems are his fault, that he is bad and worthless.

A child suffering from guilt turns away from people. He becomes afraid of authority figures such as teachers and other adults. He has been taught not to trust, to be afraid. If his own parents hit him, what unknown terrible things will strangers do to him? Because so much of the enjoyment of life comes from being with other people, such children as they grow to be adults always feel a loss, that they are missing out, that they are different.

Bottled-up anger can also be turned by the body into physical problems. A businessman who is trying to control the hectic activities of a giant company can develop stomach ulcers from his job. Children as young as seven and eight have also gotten ulcers trying to control the hectic emotions in their world. Other stress-related physical problems are headaches, stuttering, stomachaches, asthma, chest pain. Recent scientific studies have shown that the immune system, the body's ability to fight off disease, is weakened when a lot of stress is put on a person. Anger, hate, guilt, fear don't cause colds and the flu, but these strong emotions may destroy the body's ability to fight off germs and viruses.

These emotions can be handled in two ways besides trapping them inside: cleaning them out of your system entirely or turning them into another emotion that can be safely let out.

Catharsis—which means "to cleanse" in Greek—is the term psychologists use to describe getting rid of pent-up feelings. It's like sweeping the trash and cobwebs out of an attic. Screaming, yelling, and crying are all forms of catharsis. Of course, you can't use those in an abusive home where your feelings must be suppressed. You've been trained too well to keep things in. The environment won't let you release. The way to use catharsis is to be in a "safe" place where you can get emotional support and direction as you clean out the backlog of feelings. A professional mental health worker such as a school counselor or social worker may be able to get you into a group where you can have a chance to release those trapped feelings without hurting yourself or others.

Sublimation is another way to let out feelings of anger and fear. Sublimation means to change the energy of those strong emotions into the drive to accomplish something constructive. Many famous people have taken hurt feelings incurred when they were young and turned them into the drive, the energy to excel. Babe Ruth, the baseball star, turned the feelings of loss he experienced growing up as an orphan into the energy needed to make it to the Hall of Fame. Thomas Edison used the pain of being physically abused as a child and transformed it into the drive to invent the light bulb, motion pictures, and a thousand other inventions. You don't need to become famous, but you can use the energy of your emotions to improve your life.

These techniques of dealing with feelings will work only if you are safe enough to use them. No one has the right to abuse you physically. "Spare the rod, spoil the child," is a twisted quotation from the Bible that was used in the 1800s as an excuse for beating children, locking them into workhouse prisons, and treating them worse than farm animals. We are now on the verge of the twenty-first century. If someone—anyone—abuses you, it is your right to stop them. Tell your teachers, tell your doctor or school nurse, or call the police if you have to. Do not let someone else's anger and violence ruin your life.

CHAPTER 5

Sexual Abuse—
What Is Love?

Sexuality is a part of each human being. Sex is neither bad or good. It is, as they say, a fact of life. Sex is a very powerful emotional drive. The primary purpose of sex is to make babies. The fact that there are over four billion people in the world is proof of how successful nature has been with sex.

Sex can be used to express love, the attraction between a man and woman. It can be a deep sharing of closeness and pleasure. Sex can strengthen the bond between two people, giving satisfaction and a way of saying, "I share my life with you."

Sexuality can be the basis of attraction between two people. "Animal magnetism," some people call it. It is what sparks the wolf whistles at the street corner and what makes girls and guys ogle each other at the beach. It is the pure expression of sexuality, desire without love, physical attraction without emotional commitment. It is testimony to the power of sex. This desire once satisfied evaporates. The attractiveness of the object of desire is gone.

Sexual desire and love are the subject of hundreds of rock-and-roll songs, movies, and novels. Sex soaks into our daily lives from radio, magazines, and TV. Sexual images are found not only in magazines like *Playboy*. Pick up a women's fashion magazine and study the advertisements. Many of them in words and images suggest that your sexual attractiveness can be immediately improved—if you buy the advertiser's product. A fact of the advertising industry is summarized in two words: Sex sells. The power of the sex drive is abused to sell anything from cars to cigarettes to cologne. The message is that it's cool to be sexy.

That would be a small price to pay if the abuse of sex were only titillating unwary shoppers into buying products they don't need. Unfortunately sexuality, for all its high joy, pleasure, and love, has a dark side. Sex can be used to exert power.

Sex as power is not a human invention. Naturalists see it in the animal kingdom. You can see it in the nature shows on TV. For example, the bull elk shows his dominance by controlling the breeding of a harem of does. The greater his power, size, and strength, the larger the number of females with which he mates.

In human society power can be expressed in many ways. The powerful—and those who would like us to think they're powerful—flaunt their expensive homes, fast cars, and big paychecks. People make and spend more money to display success and power. Society says it is good to be powerful.

Those two messages, sex and power, can get twisted together. Then the prime energy of sex and the forceful-ness of power combine to become violence. Forcible rape is one form of sex used to gain personal power. Most authorities agree that rape is not uncontrollable sexual desire. It is not, as a recent rapist-murderer claimed in his trial, rough sex. Rape is sex used to hurt, to humiliate, to control. Victims are people that the rapist thinks of as weak, not necessarily as sexually desirable. The victims may be children or old women or other men. Many rapists admit during psychological counseling that they felt no sexual desire at all for their victims. They wanted to attack them, to force their victims to do their will. Rapists tend to be men of low self-esteem who push others down to make themselves feel tall. The feeling soon passes, but the victims may carry the humiliation and scars of the attack for the rest of their lives.

In the dysfunctional home the sexual abuser can be the mother, father, older brother, or another person in the household. One of the purposes of the abuse is to show control. The abuser gains power over the victim, who is reduced to nothing more than a thing, a piece in the perverted game played by the abuser. The abuser gains and the victim pays.

Tomika was removed from the family that allowed her to be abused only after years of incest. This is her story.

I love my Daddy. Maybe this whole thing wouldn't have happened if I had not loved him so much, or if I had let him love me less.

He called me Princess and read fairy stories to me. I would sit on his lap after I got my PJs on at bedtime. He read about castles and dragons and used my name for the princess in each story. I grew up hearing about "The Beauty Tomika and the Beast" and "Tomika and the Seven Dwarfs." I would hug him good night so tight I thought I'd break.

At five years old I began to feel that something

wasn't right at our house. Mommy and Daddy would argue when she got home from work. The arguments would go on late into the night. Mommy nagged and nagged, then Daddy would yell at her and she'd yell back, calling him names. Their shouts would get louder and louder. Then Daddy would bang out the back door and drive away.

Daddy was a sailor in the Navy when my little sister Sally was born. I remember a special day when we drove to the city to see Daddy's ship come into the harbor. It looked like a little gray toy at first, then got bigger and bigger. We drove to the dock. Sally was still a baby. She cried when the ship blew its deep horn. I covered my ears with both hands. Daddy came down the ramp of the ship, wearing a white suit and carrying a big bag over his shoulder like Santa Claus. I kissed him and kissed him. He picked me up and held me in his strong arms while Mommy held Sally.

He told us on the way home that he had quit the Navy and wouldn't be leaving us anymore. I remember being so happy when I heard that. He said he would get a job in town but that he wanted to take some weeks off first. We would take a vacation. Mommy said that was a great idea.

That night I got to stay up late because Daddy was home. I sat on his lap watching game shows while Mommy put Sally to bed. He said I was prettier than Vanna White. I gave him a big kiss. He began to tickle me, but Mommy called that I was too noisy while she was trying to get Sally to sleep. Daddy told me to shush and held me close. I fell asleep as he rubbed my back and tummy. I felt so warm.

People picked on Daddy. We went to visit Grandma Elly for a vacation. I liked to visit there because I
could play with her cat Silver. I was playing "get the
string" with him quietly on the porch when I heard
Grandma Elly talking in an angry voice with Daddy.
She said he shouldn't have quit the Navy. He told her
not to worry, he'd get a job. She kept talking to him,
but Silver ran out into the yard so I had to follow him.

We drove home that afternoon. I sat in the back
seat with Sally, who fell asleep right away. Nobody
talked. Mommy turned on the radio, and I dozed off
watching the telephone poles zoom by.

Daddy got a few jobs after that, but he never kept
one for long. He said it was because people didn't like
us. Mommy said it was because he was lazy. At the
kitchen table after lunch one day she started to pick
on him. She said the one time she needed him to
depend on, he wasn't there for her. She got real mad
and said she'd have to get a job because he was a lazy
good-for-nothing. He tried to talk to her, but Sally
began to cry. Mommy said, "See what you've done!"
and took Sally into the other room. I sat there, a big
lump in my throat. Daddy held my hand. "It's okay,
Princess," he said. "If Mommy goes to work I'll be
home with you."

The next week Mommy did get a job. Her first day
she combed her hair a hundred times and left a list of
things for Daddy to do at home. She said she'd have to
wear the pants in the family. She worked hard, and
when she came home she was tired.

Daddy took care of Sally and me. He was a good
cook because he learned in the Navy. He'd clean the
living room, wash the dishes, and then watch TV. At

first he would call around to see if he could find a job, but then he quit doing that. I told him to stay home and take care of us.

Mommy kept on working. She said working was good for her because it got her out of the house. I missed her at first, but she would bring us special presents every Friday. She'd still yell at Daddy and call him names when she thought we weren't listening. It made me mad when she picked on Daddy. I told him that, but he said I was nice to him and that was what was important, that we loved each other.

Mommy had to work late on Tuesdays. That was our special time because Daddy would get us ready for bed. He'd give Sally her bath first and put her to bed. Then I would get a long soapy bath. With a towel warmed by the heat register he rubbed me dry while I watched the water whirlpool down the drain. He rubbed between my legs and tickled me.

One night Daddy made a big bubble bath for me. He washed me up, and then he took off his clothes and got in the tub with me. We played "slippery porpoises," a game he made up. After we were done with the bath he read me a story about a princess. He told me not to tell Mommy or Sally about our bath together because they might be jealous. I was his special girl.

As I grew older I got a lot more attention. Daddy would give me a bigger dessert, or he would give me a present when I knew Sally didn't get one. Sometimes it made me feel uncomfortable the way he touched me, but he said it was a man's way to show how much he loved me.

Sally saw the unfair way we were treated and resented it. I wanted to talk to her, to tell her the price

I paid for those extra pieces of candy and toys. But I couldn't because Daddy had said to keep it a secret. Sally avoided me when we walked home from school. She was hurtful toward me. She told lies about me to my friends. I cried, but there was nothing I could do. Daddy was the only one who loved me.

I wanted to tell him to stop, but I couldn't because he's my Daddy. You must honor your father and mother. That's what they teach us at Sunday School. Mommy, Daddy, Sally, and I always got dressed up Sunday mornings to go to church.

Sundays weren't that much fun at our house. Daddy would watch sports on TV and drink beer. Mommy would be fussing around trying to get our clothes straight for the week, complaining that she couldn't work all week and be expected to get things done around the house. After a boring afternoon we went to bed early for school the next day.

On a cold Sunday night I woke up with Daddy in my bed. His rough hands rubbed on me. He smelled like beer and cigarettes. I pretended I was asleep even though it hurt. Then he gave me a big kiss and went to his room. I lay in the dark, afraid.

The next day when I was about to leave for school he gave me five dollars for being a good girl. This happened over and over. I think he was trying to keep me quiet. I don't know if Mommy knew or not. I tried to tell her that Daddy made me feel funny when he touched me. She said a little girl shouldn't feel that way about her own father. She made me feel that I was wrong. I never mentioned anything to her again.

I began doing more and more of the sweeping and mopping around the house. If Mommy needed things sewn she brought them to me. I got everyone's breakfast and made lunches for Sally and me to take to school and Mommy to take to work. It was expected of me.

Daddy stopped coming to my room after I turned twelve years old. I still did all the housework, but I felt relieved that I wasn't being bad anymore.

I didn't have any friends. A few girls invited me to play at their houses when I was in elementary school, but Mommy wouldn't let me. I didn't want anybody over to our house. They might be able to tell by seeing our home what Daddy did with me. I learned to keep people at a distance until they stopped trying to be friendly and left me alone.

JoAnna was my only friend. She never tried to butt in. Just the opposite of me, she was popular and friendly with everyone. She never tried to push me into breaking family rules about visiting others or having people over.

Everyone liked JoAnna, even the teachers in middle school. Her thirteenth birthday was the last week before Christmas vacation. She and her parents planned a super big party. They were even going to have a rock band. Everyone would be dressed up. I really wanted to go. My parents knew JoAnna, so I thought it would be okay with them.

When I got home I told Mommy and Daddy about the party. Daddy got real quiet. He asked if there were going to be boys there. Of course, I said, all the cool kids would be there, and I was invited too. No, he said, I could not go.

I started to argue. Tears filled my eyes, and my throat felt tight. I dashed to my room and slammed the door. I couldn't go! The one time I got invited somewhere, they stomped on my plans. I cried myself to sleep. I felt empty and hurt.

The party came and went. Everyone talked about how great it had been. I avoided everyone. I went to school, came home, did my work around the house, and went to bed. Everything felt cold and gray. Christmas passed. I didn't have the usual warm feelings when the tree was all dressed up in lights. Even Christmas Eve when we opened our presents just seemed like a ritual. School started again, and I went through the motions of going to classes every day and keeping to myself. I had more and more work to do at home.

On a cold afternoon I came into the house from shoveling the sidewalk to get an extra scarf. As I opened the closet door Sally suddenly came out of the bathroom, gave me a funny, frightened look, and hurried into her bedroom. A moment later Daddy came out of the bathroom tucking his shirt in. He looked surprised to see me. I grabbed my scarf and ran outside.

I couldn't let this go on. He had stopped with me, but now he had started on Sally. I breathed so fast the cold air made my chest hurt. I threw the shovel down and ran the three blocks to JoAnna's house. She was surprised to see me but invited me in. I told her I had to talk to her, she was my only friend. Someone was abusing my little sister, I told her. I cried and admitted it was my Daddy. I cried and cried and cried. All the years of secrets came out. I couldn't stop. Her mom came into the bedroom and without saying a word held me while I sobbed. I told her everything I hadn't told anyone before. She said that what Daddy had done was wrong, that it wasn't my fault but we had to stop him.

I was terrified when the police came to our house. Daddy's eyes got real big. Sally started to cry and said she didn't tell. A policewoman stayed with us while other cops took Daddy away. We could see a crowd of neighbors outside watching.

Mommy screamed at me when she got home. She told the policewoman I had made up the whole story. She called me vengeful, saying I made up the story because I couldn't go to a party. Sally said I was jealous.

I couldn't believe it! They defended Daddy! I was afraid Mommy would hurt me. Another woman from the court came and said Sally and I could live somewhere else until this was cleared up. Sally didn't want to leave home, but I did. I stayed with Mr. and Mrs. Billings, a foster family. I switched schools because everyone looked at me funny and giggled behind my back. The people from the court say Daddy probably won't have to go to prison, but he'll be on probation and have to see a psychiatrist. I will get to choose whether to live at home or with a foster family.

I am getting better grades at my new school. The Billingses don't love me—I know that—but they are kind to me and give me a safe home. They say that when I pick my permanent foster home I can stay with them.

I think I will.

The number of reported cases of sexual abuse has increased 200 percent in the last fifteen years. People are beginning to believe children when they say they have been sexually abused. States are passing laws requiring public employees—teachers, nurses, doctors—to report suspected cases of abuse, including sexual abuse.

A strong taboo has existed against thinking that children could be involved with sex, especially with their own parents. Sigmund Freud, father of psychiatry, thought that patients who told about being sexually abused as children were twisting the facts in their imaginations. But he did realize that immature sexual feelings do play a part in children's development. Part of his theory is that all little children would like to marry the parent of the opposite sex when they are two or three years old. This is called the Oedipus complex, after the story of Oedipus Rex, a Greek king who killed his father and married his mother.

Some seductive play is a normal part of growing up. Children "try out" skills they will need as adults. The home should be a safe place to practice ways of dealing with the real world. You've seen cute pictures of a preschooler giving his mother a handful of flowers: That is how a kid learns to court a member of the opposite sex. If she says, "You'll be as handsome as your daddy when you grow up," she acknowledges him and his effort to "win" her while firmly keeping him in his place in the family. He is encouraged to identify with his father as a model for the role he will play in the future.

The insecure mother who responds not as an adult but at the child's level uses the child to fulfill her own unmet needs. This causes more hurt for her, because a child cannot give emotional support to an adult. It hurts the child because by "winning" the competition for his mother's affection he loses his father as a model, and he fails to grow independently.

An eight-year-old victim of five years of sexual abuse by her stepfather was placed in a series of foster homes. After a week or two in a new foster home she would begin to make embarrassing sexual advances to the foster father in public. Acting like a prostitute had won her acceptance and affection from her stepfather. She had never learned any other ways to show affection, express friendship, or seek attention. Her story eventually ended happily when a family was found for her that kindly but firmly helped modify her behavior.

As a victim of sexual abuse you are deprived of the chance to learn how to develop relationships. You are suppressed by aggressive sexual dominance. Just at a time when you need support to grow, you are pulled down. You are not encouraged or allowed to develop a sexual identity. One is forced on you years before you are equipped to handle it. Our bodies go through stages of growth; we also mature through stages of psychological growth. These psychological stages of growth begin at birth and continue until death.

The first stage begins in infancy. During the first eighteen months of life each person must build trust. That gives a person hope. If many unhappy things happen to an infant he learns fear, feels discomfort, and develops mistrust that will last the rest of his life. Each stage of life is like a balancing act between opposites.

Young children between three and five gain self-control and cooperativeness, or they become defiant or overreact in trying to keep rules. From six to twelve kids build a sense of being able to do things, of following through on jobs. If they don't mature that way, they fall into a pattern of withdrawal and feel inferior. The final stage before adulthood is the teen years, during which we mature our ideas about who we are and what we want to do with our abilities. If teenagers don't do this, they become confused, indecisive, antisocial.

The problem with these stages of psychological growth

is that if one stage is not completed on time the following stages are postponed. Just as in physical growth, if a stage of psychological development is not completed on time, a person grows up confused and incomplete.

Tomika's father forced her into withdrawing from the rest of the world. She maintained the secret of their relationship, doing what she was told to do because the assaults kept her from developing a sense of energy on her own. Because she didn't complete the task of psychological development, she won't be able to achieve a positive sense of who she is. She could spend the rest of her life feeling herself a victim or blaming herself for her father's crimes.

The shock of seeing her father begin to rape her sister gave Tomika enough energy to break out of the victim role she had fallen into. She could then seek help in stopping the abuse. Moving to a safe home, getting professional mental help, and doing a lot of work herself will let Tomika get back on track in her lifelong work of growth.

Tomika felt tremendous pain telling on her father. Revealing the secret hurts everyone involved. But if you don't tell, if you hold the pain inside, your growth will stop. You will feel regret, guilt, and endless shame. If this has happened to you or is still going on, act now. You've been the victim too long. Save yourself. You must let the truth be known.

CHAPTER 6

Emotional Neglect: Alone in a House Full of People

The teenagers we've met so far have been victims of active abuse in the dysfunctional home. Drug abuse, alcoholism, physical abuse, incest: These are all actions, things done to others. They are what the legal system calls acts of commission, someone commiting a crime, acting against someone else.

Another kind of crimes, more difficult to prove but just as harmful, are crimes of omission or neglect. These do harm because something is left out; help or food or medicine or love is not given. Victoria's story is about a family whose dysfunction is that they never gave the love and attention that everyone needs.

As human beings we need more than just food, water, and shelter if we are to grow up to be healthy. We have a whole set of different, but equally important, needs that must also be met. These build on each other in a predictable way from simple to complicated.

Imagine a pyramid rising into the sunshine. The pyramid is made up of building blocks like the ones you played with when you were a kid. Each level of blocks stands for a different set of human needs. Your life is spent climbing this pyramid step by step, trying to reach the highest level.

The foundation of the pyramid are the basic requirements of life: food, water, air, sleep, shelter. Needs like these must be filled or there is no life. The sides of the pyramid are so steep that you can't skip steps. You have to meet your basic needs before you can go on.

The next of the six levels of the pyramid is the need to be safe. You cannot do anything else when you are running scared. Fear stimulates your body to release chemicals such as epinephrine, which makes your heart beat faster and your muscles tense. That is great for acting in an emergency, but on a long-term basis it does not help you enjoy life. You can achieve that by having a safe place to live, by having order in your life, which allows you time to think and feel, to experience life at a calmer pace.

Being fed, sheltered, and safe allows you to meet your need for love. People need to feel that they are loved, that they belong either to a family or a group. This helps shape who you are, gives you a sense of identity. Not being able to get or give love leads to loneliness and despair.

You may know people who are stuck at this level. They are unable to go on with their life because they are isolated, on the outside looking in. They neither get love nor give love. These are lonely people who spend their lives looking for love. Just as persons on the first level who cannot get food or water are driven to commit desperate acts, even killing to meet their needs, people without love who crave a sense of belonging become desperate also. If you cannot meet your need for love in your home, you will try to satisfy it outside. We are driven by our needs. There are constructive solutions: joining a club at school, making new friends. There are destructive solutions: joining a violent gang, becoming sexually promiscuous just to feel "wanted." An unmet need absorbs tremendous amounts of energy, preventing progress to the next step.

When you feel you belong, the next level is to develop self-esteem and the feeling of recognition by others. In high school few students go to school just to study. We want others to notice us. We want praise for our accomplishments. Kids try to be class president or cheerleader or class clown or the toughest guy in the tenth grade because they want the recognition of their peers. Trying to gain this recognition can be constructive. It is what makes people want to excel, improve, succeed in any group from high school to Wall Street.

The standards by which we measure our accomplishments change: Becoming a cheerleader doesn't mean a whole lot to a woman who is trying to graduate from law school. She has substituted a new goal, becoming a lawyer, to gain recognition and success in the society of business and politics. What we value changes, but we still seek to meet the need of recognition at any age. It feels good when we gain this recognition and approval: Remember how cool you felt when you were blackboard monitor in first grade?

If you can gain the recognition of your friends, the next step on the pyramid is the need to realize your own unique potential. This means to be all you can be, to be as good as only you know you have the ability to be. To reach this level you must have completed the previous four levels. There are no shortcuts. You cannot reach your potential without feeling that what you are doing is important and worthwhile.

At this fifth level you begin to blend and balance the four major parts of your life. These are the physical side of providing your body with food, rest, and exercise; the mental side of gaining knowledge and exercising your problem-solving skills; the emotional side of balancing love and anger; and the spiritual side of being creative, exuberant, and spirited. Each part of you works together with the others. You don't have to be a brain surgeon or high-powered lawyer to meet your need of fulfilling your potential. Every person's possibilities are different. A person who is a very good carpenter, telephone operator, or student meets this human requirement by doing the best he can; by balancing the body, mind, emotions, and spirit he is able to meet his own potential.

Again, remember that the only way to reach the final level is to take the earlier steps. This makes perfect sense: You cannot feel safe if you are having trouble breathing. You can't give love if you are afraid for your safety. If you are not loved you will have low self-esteem, and if you are without self-esteem there's no way you can live up to your highest potential.

What satisfies your needs changes as you grow up. When you were a child the teacher's attention was enough to meet your need for recognition. Now you need the recognition and companionship of friends your own age to fill the need. A baby needs only his parents' love; now you need to feel loved by a boyfriend or girlfriend.

The final human requirement is to search for and find beauty. Because a young child's other basic needs are so easily met, they reach the top of their needs more frequently. The whole world is new to their eyes; they see beauty in the simplest things. Watch a little kid at Christmas or on the Fourth of July. Remember how you felt about the first rainbow you saw or the glow of candles on your birthday cake. We spend the rest of our life trying to recapture that sense of fascination, allurement, and beauty.

A dysfunctional family does not allow its members to meet their needs. They become stuck at the low levels of the pyramid, unable to climb higher.

An abusive family keeps its children at the first or second level where they may not get enough food, shelter, security, or safety. Love and a feeling of belonging, halfway up the climb, are rarely obtained. That is why children of dysfunctional families have a poor self-image. They feel they don't belong with others. They become isolated and cannot live up to their potential. Excitement in discovering the world becomes, at best, floating memories of a time when they were very young. It creates a deep inner sadness that is only worse during the holidays.

Victoria, or as she prefers to be called, Vicki, grew up with all her physical and intellectual needs met. Her parents' idea of good food was a catered meal for fifty guests; their idea of basic shelter was a twenty-room house on a lake. Education for their child was so important that they moved to a city halfway across the country so that Vicki could go to the "best" private school. Most people who knew Vicki thought she had it made. Then why was Vicki so unhappy? This is her story.

No one yelled in my house. No one cried. It was unusual to hear anyone laugh. I don't remember hearing my parents argue. Everything was under control at all times.

My father was—is—a "success." His business grows day by day. I see his name in the newspaper more than I see him at home. Once when I asked him why he was always away, he answered, "I'm doing all this for you." That kept me shut up for a long time. He sacrificed his time for me. I was in his debt. I had no right to complain.

My mother is a beautiful woman. It's not just because I'm her daughter that I say that. She's tall and thin; people think she's my sister. She's an interior designer and has her own business. When people say our house looks like a million dollars, my father jokes that that's about what it cost.

Because both my parents worked, baby-sitters or housekeepers took care of me when I was little. They read to me and let me help make lunch, but I always spent a lot of time by myself, looking at books, playing in my room, watching TV.

When I was two or three the baby-sitters would spank me when I did things I wasn't supposed to do, but my parents just expected me to be perfect. No one ever yelled at my house. I felt that everything my parents did was right and to get upset was wrong. Being at home with my parents was like living in a museum where all our feelings were kept in storage.

My brother Brad was no help. He is four years younger than I and thoroughly spoiled. I know they favor him. "A boy has so much more potential than a girl," I heard my father say one time.

My best friend in elementary school was Ginny Patrillo. In fourth grade I once stayed overnight at her house. Ginny's mom stayed at home with Ginny's little brother and sisters. Her father ran a construction company. When Ginny and I came into the house after school her mom gave her a big hug and kiss. I was afraid she was going to kiss me too, but she didn't. Ginny and I played in the room that she shared with one of her sisters until her dad got home for dinner.

Everybody talked so loud at the table that it sounded like a big fight. The food tasted too spicy. I kept real quiet throughout the evening. Everyone laughed and joked around. We watched TV, and Ginny's little brother and sisters climbed on their dad's lap. He'd hug them, and they'd nuzzle up against him like he was a big teddy bear.

The next day was Saturday, and I felt relieved when Mr. Patrillo dropped me off at home at ten o'clock. My father was still asleep. My mother sat at her desk working on business. She asked how my visit was. I said fine, and she went back to work. I went up to my room and watched cartoons, grateful that my house was not crazy like Ginny's, but a little envious of all the love her parents gave.

At holidays my parents entertained friends and clients. For weeks ahead my mother supervised decorating the house, rearranging or buying new furniture. She spent a lot of time getting the house ready for the crowds who would visit during the holiday parties.

The parties were terrific. When I got older I would get dressed up in a new dress and help greet the guests at the door. How spectacular everyone looked. The women wore jewels and beautiful fur coats. Everyone ooh'd and aah'd over me, telling my parents what a beauty I would grow up to be. I would smile and curtsy. After all the guests had arrived, I would be sent to my room. My brother also was paraded at these parties. Like prized possessions, we smiled and bowed.

As I grew older school became more important to me. I felt that I had to get all As to please my parents. I spent my evenings studying. I felt awful if I missed one question on a math test. The other girls in junior high went out for cheerleading or sang in the choir. I don't know how they had time for that.

Before a big test in ninth-grade algebra I dreamed that the teacher handed out the test papers to everyone in gym class. In my dream we sat on the floor in our gym uniforms to take the test. Suddenly the test changed into one about Chapter 13. I knew I had only studied to Chapter 10. I felt sweat on my palms. I tried to figure out the problems, but they didn't make sense. Everytime I wrote down a number it changed. Everyone handed in their tests. My stomach hurt. I felt as if I had to go to the bathroom real bad. When the teacher blew her whistle, I woke up. I couldn't breathe. I ran into the bathroom and threw up.

My mother saw the light and came in to ask if I was okay. I told her I must have eaten something that disagreed with me. She gave me an antacid and went back to bed. I lay in bed not daring to go back to sleep, afraid of what dreams I might have. I don't know why I didn't tell my mother about my nightmare. It was easier to make up an excuse. It is important in our house not to have bad feelings. It wasn't okay even to be scared.

My parents rush through their busy lives, doing what has to be done, every moment planned. When they're not at work they are at community fundraising meetings. Even our leisure time is scheduled, planned so that no one has to talk to anyone else about anything important.

I am the only one in my family who has bad feelings, but I push them away and hide them because I am childish. My mother never cries. My father never raises his voice. All our feelings are smothered.

Everything's nice. Everything was fine until I fell in love.

Dave entered my life like sunshine in my sophomore year of high school. His black wavy hair framed his always smiling face. I felt I could melt whenever I saw him walking in the hall. Our only class together was third-hour English. One class project was to write a report on a Shakespeare play with a partner. Dave asked me to work with him! This would be the best term paper ever!

We were to read *Hamlet* and write a report together. Dave invited me to his house on Saturday afternoon to work on the paper. I spent all night Friday memorizing as much as I could. I had the paper almost written when I got to his house. Dave was impressed when I quoted:

> Doubt thou the stars are fire;
> Doubt that the sun doth move;
> Doubt truth to be a liar;
> But never doubt I love.

We read several scenes together. He said I should be an actress. We added a little more to the report, and I said I would type it up for class. He said thanks and walked me home. I would have kissed him goodbye, but I just smiled and said "Bye."

I felt I was floating. My mother wasn't home and the housekeeper was vacuuming for the party that night, so I went to my bedroom and typed.

Usually I have trouble getting my assignments done on time, even though I spend so much time studying. I'll start a paper and get it half written, then begin to worry that the teacher won't like it or that it's stupid.

I'll tear it all up and start all over again, or I'll just stare at the pages thinking that there is no way I can get all my work done. What happens either way is that the work gets pushed to the last minute and I'm always in a panic to get things done. At least this paper was turned in on time.

I spent the next two weeks hoping that Dave would ask me out, but he didn't. I saw him in the hall between classes, but he was always with his buddies and never saw me. Many times I thought maybe I should telephone him. A couple of times I even dialed the number but hung up before the phone rang.

One week I didn't see him in class. I began to worry that he'd been in a terrible accident or something. Finally I asked one of his friends if anything had happened to Dave. He looked at me like I was stupid. "He moved to Chicago last week," he told me and walked away.

I felt as if the ceiling had fallen on me. I had dreamed that I could love this guy forever, and he left without even saying good-bye. It must have been my fault. I should have—what? I didn't know what I had done wrong, but I would never love another guy. When I got home I put on my black jeans and black turtleneck. I would wear black in mourning for the true love that died before it could be born.

Others noticed my sorrow, I'm sure, but no one ever said a word about it. Day after day I wore black, a black sweater or scarf or black earrings. My parents didn't say anything. They were so busy that I couldn't interupt them with my sorrow. Besides, what could they do? I pretended everything was fine, smiled politely to guests, and spent most of the time in my room. My only chance for love had escaped me.

Later in the year my English teacher must have seen how much pain I covered with my cheerful face. He suggested that I try out for the school play. I picked up a copy of the play, *The Miracle Worker*, and took it home to read. I read it all the way through before dinner time. The lead role was for a girl. I found that the character's lines expressed my own feelings of frustration and loneliness. I practiced saying some of the speeches in front of the mirror. I could do this.

My mother was home for dinner that night. I told her I thought I might try out for the play. She said it was a good idea but not to be too disappointed if I didn't get a part. I agreed with her, but deep down I thought I would show her. I would be the best. My brother was rooting for another girl to get the lead and said I didn't have a chance.

I read for the lead role at the tryouts. I didn't even want to be considered for anything less. I was a nervous wreck but determined, and I got it! I knew I had to work really hard now. I came to rehearsals early and stayed late. I memorized not only my lines but everyone else's lines too. I used a tape recorder and played it back to get just the right tone of voice for each speech. Some of the other kids goofed around at rehearsals; it really ticked me off. They'd pay attention when *I* took the stage.

In a scene at the beginning of the play I had a speech about how bad my childhood was. Even during rehearsals I could make real tears appear in my eyes. "Vicki, how do you do that?" the other kids would ask. I'd say I just thought of sad things. I could tell that they were impressed, but I didn't gloat. In fact, I kept separate from the others. After rehearsals they would go out for pizza. I'd stay around to help the director, or go straight home to brush up on my lines.

I helped with anything involved with the play. I painted scenery. I sold advertising for the playbill, I sold tickets door-to-door.

The play was to run for three nights. I bought front-row opening night tickets for my parents. Opening night came, and I left early to get my makeup on. My mother was still with a client, and my father wasn't home yet. At the theater the rest of the cast were nervously joking around backstage. I put on my make-up slowly, thinking about how I would feel tonight. The girls in the dressing room were chattering back and forth making plans for the cast party, but I didn't get involved with that. Tonight I had to make the play perfect.

Everything went well. One of the guys forgot part of his lines, but I was able to cover so hardly anybody knew. But when I looked out over the audience my parents' seats in the front row were empty.

Afterwards everyone's friends, parents, aunts and uncles came backstage to congratulate them. People, some strangers, started to tell me what a wonderful job I'd done, but I excused myself and hid in the bathroom. I didn't want to talk to anyone or hear their words of praise. I avoided making eye contact with anyone for fear they could see how sad I felt when I should be proud of a job well done. I couldn't bear to smile back at them. I couldn't bear being reminded that my own parents didn't show up. I don't have parents, I thought. They are not here for me. I am an emotional orphan. Could anyone see that in my eyes?

When I got home there were two messages on the

telephone answering machine, one from my mother about how her client's business took longer than she expected, and one from my father saying he was sorry he couldn't make it to the play but he was called out of town. My brother had football practice that he couldn't miss.

I couldn't talk to the machine, I couldn't yell at it, cry on its shoulder. I erased the messages. The housekeeper had made a snack for me, but I wasn't hungry. I suddenly felt very tired. I excused myself and went to bed between cold sheets in a cold room in a cold, cold house. The house was empty and so was I—and so I cried.

Cold is a good description of Vicki's house. Without the ups and downs of emotional involvement, the four parts of the whole person become unbalanced. Her parents traded their daughter for their careers. In their own minds they felt they were giving Vicki everything money could buy, and they were. However, they stole from Vicki their time.

Recently the phrase "quality time" has became popular with working parents who leave their children, some as young as six weeks, in the care of low-paid baby-sitters. "Quality time" is supposed to mean that these parents make up for this abandonment by compressing all the affection and attention their children need into the few hours they spend with them in the evenings and on week-ends. That way they can keep their career and not feel guilty about leaving their children each day.

There is no such thing as "quality time"; there is only time. Parents have to *be there* for their children when the kids need encouragement or love. The little kid who falls and scrapes his knee can't wait for love and kisses until six o'clock when Mommy gets home. He needs the warm reassurance of his parents now. Studies show that children separated from their parents, even in approved foster homes, have many of the same problems handling their emotions and dealing with other people as do children of alcoholic families.

A child growing up in a dysfunctional family has frequent intense nightmares. Anxiety causes nightmares. Your mind tries to get rid of the feelings of uncertainty by burying them under other thoughts. At night those feelings are played back, but they are distorted and twisted so that your mind doesn't recognize them for what they are. All you feel is the scariness.

Growing up, you thought you were the direct cause of your problems. All little kids feel responsible for actions that are really beyond their control. To try to control those anxious feelings you may become a perfectionist, a person who tries to do everything exactly right. Maybe that will make the problems go away. Of course, there is no way you can be perfect, and the problems are still there, so you begin to judge yourself without mercy. Nothing you do is ever good enough in your eyes. You have low self-esteem.

You have difficulty following through on projects, whether it's a school assignment or even a hobby. You do your schoolwork at the last minute because you keep putting it off, changing it, waiting for the "right" time or to be "in the mood" to work on it. You probably have half-completed stamp collections or paintings or model ships tucked away somewhere, projects that you began with enthusiasm but that soon fell by the wayside.

You overreact. As soon as a problem arises you feel like giving up. A clerk in a store at the mall is rude to you, and you refuse ever to go there again. If a friend doesn't invite you to a party, you might never speak to him again. Under this brusque exterior you feel guilty, though, that you are somehow to blame for the problem. Because of your home life you don't know what normal behavior is. You take yourself very seriously. You watch every move you make. You think about past "mistakes" you've made, turning them over and over in your mind. You are hard on yourself and allow no self-pity.

You read this now thinking, "They're right. I am all those terrible things!" *It's not your fault.* How could you know what normal is, raised in the crazy house you lived in? How could you develop a sense of safety and self-esteem when your basic needs were not being met? Congratulate yourself: You have learned to cope with anger, broken promises, lies, silence. Think of that as an accomplishment, not a condemnation. You have grown up in a personal hell and survived.

To make it, you've had to build yourself a suit of armor. You need it. You need the shield of denial to protect yourself. You have a sharp sword to cut the lies that wrapped around you. You have put on a helmet of responsibility because in a house without true parents, true support, you've had to become responsible for yourself and them. You have a breastplate of cold steel—trustlessness—to protect your heart.

You built this armor piece by piece as you grew up. You needed to protect yourself, to fulfill your need for safety. But now that you are grown it will begin to weigh you down. It will be hard to climb higher on the pyramid of needs. You will use up too much energy with each step. You have to leave some of the armor behind.

The next chapters will show you ways of coping with your dysfunctional family. Some will work better in your life than others. But none of them will work if you don't give them a chance.

There is an old saying: Today is the first day of the rest of your life. You cannot make your family and private history disappear. Trying to do so will use up a life of energy. But you don't have to drag them around with you forever. Your new life, your free life, is beginning now.

CHAPTER 7

Sending Out

Calls for Help

D id you begin to recognize yourself in the previous chapters? Families are supposed to give
support to everyone in the family. No matter
whether the family is made up of six kids and a mother,
father, and grandparents living in a big farmhouse or a
divorced mother and her daughter in a small urban apartment, the reason for being part of a family is to give and
receive support as you build your life.

You've met five families that have broken down. Because
of alcohol, drugs, physical and sexual abuse, and emotional
neglect, these families are not working. They are dysfunctional. Not only do they not give support to the members of
the family, but they rip away what little support there is.
As a child growing up in such a dysfunctional family you
are the one who suffers the most. It is your future that is
being ruined. You cannot change the past, but you will let
it ruin your life unless you begin to deal with it now.

The first part—the hardest part—is deciding that you

need help. You can help yourself, or you can ask for help from others. But until you admit that there is a problem in your family, *there can be no help.* Even if the abuse stops, the pain will go on. Your family will not magically heal itself. If you are not part of the solution, you will be part of the problem. But how do you cope?

Dysfunctional families are famous for denying that there is a problem. Denial is one of the ways human beings try to handle pain, whether it is physical or emotional. A teenage boy will angrily deny that his mother sexually abused him when he was little, even though he remembers its happening. He thinks the memories are just remembered dreams, "nightmares" that haunt him. They are nightmares, but they are real. By denying the reality, he puts the blame on himself for her actions and lives in painful guilt.

A little girl brought into the emergency room with a broken arm and bruises on her face, back, and legs told the nurse that she fell down the stairs. She repeated the story that her parents made up in the car on the way to the hospital. Her mind denies the truth as too terrible. The truth is that her parents beat her and twisted her arm behind her back until it snapped. The nurse may think that the little girl is abused, but she cannot prove it because of the denial by the whole family. After her arm was set the little girl went home with her parents. The next week they beat her because she wet the bed. Her father kept hitting her until she passed out. She died during the night, drowning in her own vomit.

Denial that there is a problem is no solution.

Another form of denial admits that there is a problem but says that nothing can be done about it. An example of this is a boy whose father was a "weekend alcoholic" who stayed drunk from Friday night to Sunday evening. During this time he terrified his family with outbursts of verbal and physical abuse. The whole family put up with this abuse for years because they thought it was unsolvable. The son went to the family minister, who told him that the beatings were the boy's "cross to bear," that sparing the rod would spoil the child, and the boy's duty was to honor his father, not accuse him. The boy gave up trying to find a way out. He denied that there was a solution to the problem.

In every dysfunctional family, no matter how terrible the abuse, there is a solution to the problem. There is hope. The solutions are not always easy, they are not always quick. But the problems you have to solve are not easy, nor did they appear overnight. Use some of the ideas in these chapters to take hold of the problem, explore the solutions, and get rid of that elephant in your living room.

When you stop denying that there is a problem and that there is a solution, you may feel guilt. Tomika felt tremendous guilt when her father molested her, thinking that it was somehow her fault that he forced himself on her sexually. Many crimes against children and teenagers stay hidden because of embarrassment. You may not want to admit to the world that there is a big problem in your family because you think people will blame you, think that you're the one who did wrong. Guilt is a very powerful emotion. It has kept people powerless, actionless, ashamed for generations. Some religions are based on guilt. Sin and damnation are taught to keep people in line. The guilt pervades people's entire lives. Even if they don't actually do something, they feel guilty for even thinking about it. Some religions build the guilt far above your personal actions and thoughts; they say you are guilty for what your relatives thought and did a thousand years ago.

You did not cause the problems in your family. It is not your fault. You are the victim. Someone did these things to you when you were a child. You are not responsible for their actions. They are the guilty ones, not you. You are, however, part of the problem now until you become part of the solution.

The next step after feeling guilty is fear. You have a lot to fear. You're afraid of what others will say when the truth comes out. You are afraid of what may become of your family if the police are called. Many of the things your parents have been doing to you are crimes that carry prison terms. You may fear for your life. Abusive parents do kill their children. In New York City it is estimated that one child is killed by his or her own parents each day.

You're afraid of change. It is scary to change the pattern you are in even though it is hateful. Because of a strong natural force called inertia, all things, once moving in one direction, tend to keep going that way. It is natural that you don't want to change.

But you will change. As your body develops from teenager to adult you are transformed. Being afraid of the changes won't stop them, but you *can* choose different ways of coping with them. You can just let them happen, let yourself be pushed around and used by your family like a little kid. You can fall into the patterns your parents have laid out and become a drunk, or a drug addict, or a child molester too.

Or you can do something about the changes that are happening. You can choose *not* to become like your parents; you can choose to have a life of your own, a free life. Remember that nothing in the universe remains constant except change. It is how you use this change that you know is going to happen that will make the difference in how you feel about the rest of your life. It is scary to change. It is more frightening to be the one who has to force the decisions of how to change. You do not have to make all these choices and decisions on your own. There are others who can help and ways to help yourself that we explore in the next chapters. All you need to realize is that change is coming and it is up to you to choose.

As you realize the tremendous damage that has been done to you by your dysfunctional family, as you look at the pain, sorrow, and guilt that have been poured over you, and as you look at the hard decisions you now must make, you may begin to be angry. That is good. Anger at your parents (for what they have done) and at yourself (for allowing it) is what will give you the energy to save yourself.

Anger, like any emotion, is neither good nor bad. Feelings just happen; we can't stop them any more than we can turn our heartbeat on and off. People who brag that they have no feelings are just covering them up. Famous actors who have spent their entire lives on TV, in movies, and on the stage admit that they still get nervous before they go on stage, even though they have done it a thousand times. People who say they have no feelings, and believe it, are lying to themselves. It is what you *do* with your feelings of anger that makes the difference between good and bad. If you try to keep them inside, they will turn into stomach ulcers or stress-related depression. Eventually these trapped and suppressed feelings will blow out without your having any control over them at all.

Use the anger to remind yourself *why* things must change. That anger will give you the strength to stand up to your tormentors. It will push you to make the hard decisions you must make about your future, your life.

You will go through these feelings of denial, guilt, fear, and anger as you take the next step in coping with your dysfunctional family. It is important to recognize these feelings when they well up inside of you. It is important to remember that they are natural and normal. Remember how to use them to set yourself free. *Denial*: Yes, there is a problem in my life. Yes, it can be fixed. *Guilt*: You are the *victim*. The things that were done to you were not your fault; you are not to blame for your parents' actions. *Fear*: President Franklin D. Roosevelt said, "We have nothing to fear but fear itself." The changes that you are going to make are scary, but there will be changes whether you want them or not. Be the one who picks the changes, not the one whom change picks on. *Anger*: Allow this natural emotion to give you the energy you need to cope with your dysfunctional family in a positive, growing, free way.

To work through these feelings, it is important that you recognize the dysfunction in your family. You need to figure out where you are in your family and how you are made a victim. To know the problem is to know the first step in solving it. You are taking on a tremendous responsibility, but responsibility means setting yourself free from others' control.

You can probably place your family in one or two of the broad categories of substance abuse, sexual abuse, physical and verbal abuse, and neglect. What are the dysfunctional actions that you must look for, react against, and plan around?

The biggest lack in all dysfunctional families is lack of communication. Communication is simply people making contact with each other. It is how we deal with other human beings. Without successful communication there is no understanding between people. It is a two-way street; you must give and receive for it to work. The truer the messages you send, the more success you will have. Good communication helps you better understand your own ideas and feelings by putting them into words and by getting feedback from others. You have grown up in a family with terrible communication skills. To get help for yourself, you need to improve your own skills first. You will need them to make your needs and concerns known to your family so that change can begin. If that doesn't work, you will need those skills to get help for yourself outside of the family.

Successful communication has four main points. The first is to make your message simple and clear. Rehearse in your mind exactly what you want to say before you open your mouth.

Timing is very important. If you try to tell your alcoholic mother why she should stop drinking at five o'clock in the afternoon when she is falling-down drunk, your message won't get through. If you try to tell a teacher whom you trust that you didn't do your homework because your father threatened to beat you if you didn't clean the basement first, don't try to do so just as the ball is ringing for class.

Don't do these things unless that *is* your message: I want to fail, I want not to be heard, I don't want help. Be honest with yourself. Know what is the message that you're trying to send. Keep it simple and clear. Be truthful.

Second, if too much information is given at once, the whole message can be lost. Did you ever have someone give you directions—turn left at the light, then three blocks left, then right—that had so much information crammed into run-on sentences that you ended up even more confused than you started? That is called overload.

Everybody has a different ability to absorb information. Be sure you are successfully communicating with someone by not overloading people with more information than they can handle. This is especially important because the facts you have to communicate are emotionally very painful. They are facts that many people don't want to hear lest they disturb their simple, unrealistic view of the world.

That brings us to the third part of good communication: flexibility. If you think the person is not getting your message, back off. Is your message simple and clear? Is this not a good time for the person really to hear what you have to say? Have you given the person too much to handle at once? You need to change what you want to say to fit the way the person is understanding.

How can you tell that what you're saying is not getting through? Look for feedback, the fourth part of communication and the most important. Feedback means that the other person sends messages back to you. It can be straightforwardly spoken: "I understand what you are saying," or by gestures such as nodding. Other messages sent without talking—called nonverbal messages or body language—are facial expressions, gestures, posture. If you talk to your parents about the amount of time they spend with you and they sit with their arms crossed, you can know that they are trying to lock themselves in, protect themselves from your words. If you talk and a person looks at you, nodding and leaning toward you, he is telling you through body language and nonverbal feedback that he understands you.

You don't need to be an expert at reading people's body language to get feedback. The simplest way to get it is to ask, "Do you understand?" That brings us back to the first parts of communication: Keep the message simple, and give it at the right time in amounts that a person can understand. Be flexible to change how you give your message, repeating or rephrasing it as necessary. Get feedback. Check to make sure that you are getting through to the other person and that you are listening to what he is saying in words and body language.

Whom do you approach in your family to begin the task

of making things better? In each dysfunctional family that we met in the earlier chapters, three people caused the dysfunction: the victim, the abuser, and the bystander. Let's look at each type of dysfunctional family more closely to identify these people and the role they played.

In the alcoholic family, Alice was the victim. Her father was the abuser, misusing not only alcohol but his whole family. The bystanders were Alice's brother, sister, and mother. These bystanders are not innocent. They are sometimes called codependents, because their lives are also dependent on the abuse. They are also called enablers, because by not admitting that a problem exists they allow or enable the abuser to continue. In some legal systems a person who stands by and does nothing while a crime is committed is as guilty as the criminal.

Several enablers figure in Barry's story about his mother's drug abuse. His father must have sensed something was different with his wife, but he did nothing. Enablers' defenses for not doing anything about the problem run the whole fence-length of denial: "I didn't know...I was too busy to notice...She never told me." All these are excuses to cover up their own part in the problem. Everyone in her family enabled Jill to kill herself even though she sent out messages that she felt suicidal. Her messages were not received because the family's ability to hear her had been destroyed by years of lack of practice. They treated Jill's troubles the way they treated all the problems in the family—by ignoring them.

Tomika's mother, by belittling and arguing with her husband, cut off communication within the family. Who wants to talk when talking leads to arguments and mean-ness? By destroying the love that should have been in the family, she enabled the incest to start. By destroying the family's ability to communicate, she enabled the incest to go on and on. Tomika's father became so used to this sick environment that he fully expected Tomika to go on being a victim even when he turned to her younger sister. He was surprised when Tomika didn't just pretend that nothing was going on.

People who enable a physical abuser to continue may be afraid that he will turn on them if they interfere or question him. They allow someone else to be beaten so they are left alone. That is called *scapegoating*: Someone takes all the blame and punishment for the whole family. It is common in abusive families. Roberto saw himself in the scapegoat role. He put up with the beatings his father inflicted on him so that his younger brothers and sisters would be left alone.

In families that abuse their children by emotional neglect, everybody involved becomes an enabler to allow the cold-blooded silence to continue. The child growing up is hurt the most because she cannot grow emotionally, her basic needs are not met. But because of the shallowness of their relationships with each other, everyone in the family is doomed to live without love.

To send out your call for help you need to communicate with both the abuser and the enablers. They all need to know the problem that is being caused, that what they are doing is out of hand, that a change has to take place for everyone's good. Things cannot remain as they are. They need to be confronted with these facts.

People sometimes think that confronting someone is a violent act like prizefighters confronting each other in a boxing ring or armies having a confrontation at a border. The confrontation we are talking about is not destructive, but rather constructive. The purpose of constructive confrontation is to focus everyone's mind on the problem. As you can see, that is just the opposite of the enabler, who denies—and helps others deny—the problems around them.

In a confrontation use "I" messages. Say what it feels like to you: "It hurts *me*...*I* cry every night..." That is not the same as blaming. Avoid "you" messages: "*You* have a problem...This is *your* fault..." That only puts everyone on the defensive and takes away the power of your confrontation.

Describe only visible behavior; talk only about things that you can actually see happening. Don't try to figure out what goes on inside the other person's head; you'll usually be wrong.

An example of describing behavior might go like this: "Dad, last night you had three drinks between the time you got home and the news came on." Those are facts that cannot be easily argued with. Compare it to this: "Dad, you get drunk every night because you can't stand us." The speaker has made an assumption about *why* his father does things. By not sticking to the visible facts, he allows his father to deny the problem. By assuming what is going on in his father's head—that he drinks because he can't stand the family—he allows his father to sidestep the issue of drinking and change the subject: "I only have a little drink because work is so stressful..." If you describe visible behaviors there will be less denial. If you try to read another person's thoughts, the person can argue that you are wrong and the confrontation becomes defensive.

To have a constructive confrontation, describe your feelings by name. This is not the time to be vague. It is the opportunity to express yourself precisely, with the strength of honesty and truth. Use feedback from the other person to make sure your message is getting across. Remember that the person has been practicing denial for years. Your words will be a shock. The person will try to misinterpret what you are saying. Repeat yourself. Clarify what you are saying: "No, Mom, I'm not saying I hate you. I said I feel that I lose out when you take those pills."

What you are doing is being assertive. Assertiveness is sometimes confused with aggressiveness. The two are not the same. Being aggressive is attacking someone. The bully on the elementary school playground is an example of someone who is aggressive. He tries to exert his will on other people. He makes himself bigger in his own mind by shoving everyone else down.

At the opposite pole from aggressive people are those who are easily manipulated. They bury their emotions and cannot stand up for their opinions or even their own needs. These people are called passive. Between the two are assertive people, who try to meet their own needs without trampling on others.

When you are assertive you stand up for yourself. Because of the way you have learned to cope in your dysfunctional family, this may be very hard for you at first. You have been taught from infancy to give in to others' needs. Trying to be a "perfect" child, you learned to judge yourself harshly for every problem that appeared, whether it was yours or really belonged to someone else. You have low self-esteem.

Assertiveness is saying to the world, "This is what I want, this is what I need." If you don't ask for what you want or need, the odds are that you won't get it. There is no guarantee that you will get it if you do ask; but by standing up for yourself and asking you show that you care about yourself and you begin to show your inner strength. You may need to make an effort to be assertive at first, but the more you practice it the more natural it will become in your daily life. Other people like to deal with those who are assertive about what they want. It eliminates having to second-guess everything they say.

Now is the time to confront your abuser. If you run into the room screaming at the top of your lungs you will gain very little. Your message will not be heard; people will simply react to your behavior. Remember, a dysfunctional family is used to craziness. Insanity is nothing new to people who ignore their children, beat their children, take drugs, have sex with their children. There's an old saying that, "All the world is crazy save you and me; and sometimes I'm not too sure about you."

Your confrontation must be planned. Don't fall into the trap that many children of dysfunctional families do: becoming so absorbed in the planning that they never get around to turning the plans into action. Remember, if you are not assertive now, the craziness of your family will haunt you the rest of your life.

Decide what specific things you want done. Make sure these are actions, behaviors you can see. That will give you a chance for success. Don't ask for a change in attitude: "I want respect..." may be exactly what you do want, but worded that way it is too vague. Can't you just hear the parent's answer: "If you want respect you'll have to earn it!" That conversation will get you nowhere fast. If you focus your assertive statement on a specific, observable behavior change you will have a better chance of achieving your goal. For example, if you say, "I don't want you to come into the bathroom when I'm taking a shower," that tells a person exactly what you want and expect; by changing the behavior you will get the change in attitude, the respect that you want as part of the bargain.

By being specific about the changes you want, you set up a contract with the other person. You are asking for changes in the way things are. You are asking for changes that can be seen. The other person will know if those changes happen.

This being specific is one of the hardest parts of the confrontation. You know that you want and need changes in your family, but you have to make known to yourself and the rest of the family exactly what those changes are. How can you figure out what they should be?

One way to get started is to make a list. A written list of what you want to change will help you get organized. To get ideas for this list, you can use a technique called brainstorming, which is writing down everything you can think of about the subject at hand as fast as possible.

When you have thought of as many things as you can, put the list away in a drawer or folder. Let it sit for a day or so. Then take the brainstorm list and a fresh piece of paper to make a more detailed list. Now is the time to think about each item on the brainstorm list. Pick out the best ideas and discard the rest. You can do this brainstorming two or three times so you will have a well-thought-out final list.

Now you are prepared to meet with those involved. This can be at the dinner table if you think that's right, or you can set up a special time and place (6:30 in the den, for example). If you think it would help to have someone from "your side" there, invite a trusted friend to be with you and explain why. This other person can act as a referee to help keep the discussion on track. Lay some ground rules at the beginning of the confrontation, but keep them simple. You might say that everything talked about at the meeting is to be confidential, and that no one can interrupt when someone is talking.

This is not the time for blaming. Avoid "you" sentences: *You* drink too much, *you* always hurt people, *you* are tearing the family apart. These just block the communication lines with anger. Avoid fault-finding: Your drugs *cause* all our problems, it's your *fault* we live in this cheap apartment. The attacked person will try to defend himself, usually with denial. Avoid predicting: We'll *never* be happy because of your drinking, you *will* ruin all our lives. That only gives the other person the chance to avoid facing the truth that you are telling. He or she will twist your words in order to deny the reality of what's going on and responsibility for his or her actions. Those actions are what you are trying to stop by confronting him or her with the truth.

By telling the abusers and enablers in your family the truth about what they are doing and have done to you, you have much to gain. You get away from the secrecy that has isolated you and helped make you a victim. Breaking the unspoken secret shatters the cycle of silence that strangles the dysfunctional family. You make it possible to take the first step in getting help for your family and yourself. You get away from denial. Facing the truth now is frightening for you and those involved, but the steps you take now will make you feel strong, proud, free.

You are in a battle now against denial, guilt, fear, and anger. If at first you don't succeed, don't give up. The behaviors did not start overnight, nor will they disappear suddenly. It will be painful, but the tumor must be removed if your family is to remain intact. Blaming your parents for what has happened to you will not solve the problem. In fact, it will cause additional problems. Perhaps it *is* your parents' fault for the way you are, but it is *your* fault if you stay that way.

CHAPTER 8

If You Can't Save Them, Save Yourself

I
n Chapter 7 we discussed constructive ways to come face to face with the source of the family problems. In this chapter we shall go one step farther and say "What about me?" The confrontation may have forced your parents (or other offending persons) to take a good look at themselves for the first time in many years. Maybe they didn't like what they saw and managed to twist the blame onto you. Adults who sexually or physically or emotionally abuse their children usually have very low self-esteem themselves and perhaps were similarly abused when they were children. But remember, their level of self-esteem and their abuse in childhood are not your fault. You are not a psychiatrist or social worker or in any way responsible for their mental well-being. We are not saying that you should verbally abuse them in return, but you must make your

clear, well-thought-out feelings known. Then wait for their reaction. If they are drunk or belligerent, it is not the *time* to confront them. In comedy as in tragedy, *timing* is very important.

So far we have lumped all the dysfunctional groups together. In this chapter we need to be more specific, because the methods of handling a confrontation and the aftermath are a little different in each case. We shall focus mainly on the abusive parent although we know that any member of the family can be abusive. If the children are using alcohol or drugs or sexually abusing someone, it is the duty of the parents to take control of the family and get professional help for the abuser and everyone else in the family who is affected. But if the parents are not taking action or are themselves the abusers, the burden of getting help falls on the children. This book is designed to help teens trapped in precisely this situation. It is not designed to speak to the needs of the parents or adults.

The first dysfunction we discussed (in Chapter 2) was *alcohol abuse.* Living with an alcoholic parent leaves a void in the middle of you. Most of the time you pretend that nothing is wrong, and when you do admit that there is a problem you look the other way and hope it will stop (but deep down you know that it won't unless you or your brothers and sisters or the enabling parent face up to it).

You probably think you know your siblings really well and know what they would say or do about confronting the alcoholic. Perhaps you don't know for sure until you talk about it. But in an alcoholic home being open and honest with anyone is simply not done. Think about what would happen if you did confess your feelings to each other. Would it turn into a sibling-rivalry shouting match? Or would it allow the younger members to express their fears and sadness and look to the older children (often teens) for help, support, and guidance. Maybe you don't want that additional burden. You have already been playing the role of mature parent to your parents, and now you are supposed to be the parent for your younger brothers and sisters. Maybe it's just too much of a load for your young shoulders to bear.

If you live near other family members who are not directly affected by the alcoholic (such as aunts, uncles, or grandparents), try talking to them. Believe it or not, they may not know how serious or long-term the problem has been. They may be aware that your father or mother drinks, but they may think of him or her only as a "social drinker," someone who drinks only at parties or on special occasions to be "friendly" or sociable. They may think, perhaps, that he or she drinks a little after a long hard day at work or before or after supper. You will have the unenviable task of describing how the alcoholic drinks on *all* of those occasions, and frequently starts drinking in the early morning and continues all day long even at work, even while driving the car.

You must let them know that what may have started as social drinking is now intensely private drinking. Tell them about those hidden bottles of vodka you find in the back of a drawer when you are putting the laundry away. Tell them about your parent's being too drunk to remember important things like birthdays or anniversaries or school events for parents. Tell them how unhealthy the alcoholic has become in body as well as mind, how he or she skips meals and often drinks on an empty stomach, has lost weight or stopped washing or wears the same clothes for days. Explain how your parent looks dazed and lost, with pathetic bloodshot eyes and pitiful stagger.

Tell them how your parents argue over the alcohol

problem constantly. Let them know that things are getting worse and worse and how it happens every single day, not just once in a while. You are frightened each night when the whole family is at home. That's when kids are in bed pretending to be asleep and the alcoholic comes home, not from work, but from the bar. That's when the angry words and accusations start to fly. That's when the threat of serious injury or death is at its peak, because you know there are knives or even a gun in the house. You worry about what would happen to you if your parents killed each other or were sent to prison for murder. These are certainly not visions of sugarplums dancing in your head as you try to go to sleep. As the arguments escalate, you hope and pray that they will stop fighting and go to bed. You are tense and ready to jump up and run to help whoever is injured if a scuffling match begins with slapping or punching or things being thrown. Tell them how you cry, but not out loud. Tell them how you keep the tears inside because you have to be strong to help the others and not let the offender know he or she is hurting *you*. Tell them how much it hurts—they don't know.

Now let's look at the parent who is a *drug abuser*. Many of the patterns described for alcoholics are true of drug users, because alcohol is as much a drug as cocaine or heroin. These drugs (and all the other "social" drugs) affect the central nervous system and, more important, the brain. The user gradually becomes unable to think of anything but getting more of the substance and easily slips into daily use.

With crack cocaine the problem is even worse; after only one hit of the drug your body (especially the brain) is not able to deny the desire for more and you are addicted.

Your life begins a steep downward spiral. Nothing else matters but getting the drug. It is a sad and desperate state for the user and totally destructive of the family unit. Only professional health-care providers can reverse the effects of the drug, and that only if the abuser agrees to seek help and after much time and money are spent in treatment.

While it is true that drugs like marijuana are not as addictive as cocaine, they are at least as habit-forming as cigarettes, which also cause severe illness and death. Many people innocently begin smoking and then find that they can't quit, not because they are weak or lack willpower but because a physical addiction to the drug nicotine has taken place. You may think it is silly to compare drug and alcohol abuse to cigarette smoking, but they are all powerful drugs. From caffeine and nicotine to marijuana and cocaine, our culture is saturated with chemical dependency, both legal and illegal.

Teens who know that their parents use illegal drugs are torn between loyalty to the family and fear that the parents will be hurt or arrested or even killed if they are dealing drugs to others. As with alcohol abuse, the first question to ask yourself is, "Do I feel safe in this family?" If your answer is "No," and you feel threatened either physically or emotionally, you need to take action. Without knowing the details of your case, we cannot give specific advice. We recommend calling a crisis intervention hotline (see the list in the Appendix). You can talk anonymously to the person who answers, giving the details and considering your options. Maybe the best thing to do in your case is nothing, but at least you have expressed your troubling thoughts to someone who understands people in your situation and perhaps can give you some insightful advice.

*   *   *

In a family suffering *physical abuse* the need-to-tell the family's secret to someone cannot be greater. Parents who are hitting, slapping, kicking, or in any other way hurting their children must be reported. We know it is not easy to share this dark secret, but you must do it to make it stop. It will never stop by itself. Parents who hit their children as an easy outlet for their anger were probably abused when they were young. So the idea of going to grandparents or aunts and uncles may not work if they too are abusers or were abused. They don't know how to be kind, gentle, and understanding because they were never taught how. The only childrearing they know is how they were treated as children, and all too often they fall into those same hateful ways, even though they remember how much it hurt as a child.

Okay, you cannot talk to anyone in the family, and we understand why. What do you do? Whom can you turn to? Perhaps if you have a religious influence in your life, you could talk to a minister, priest, or rabbi. Another possible source of support might be a professional such as a doctor, nurse, social worker, coach, or teacher. But remember that in some states these people are required by law to report cases of child abuse, or even suspected cases. The police must then investigate and attempt to gather evidence to support the claim of physical abuse. If you do not want legal action, you will have to talk to someone else. The laws were enacted to protect children from abusive parents and, if needed, to remove the children from the home and place them in foster care. You may thinking that you do not want to be taken away from your home and put with strangers, but remember that no matter what you did wrong, you do not deserve to be beaten. If your mother or other enabling adult is also being abused, you might try to persuade her to seek help. People in this position often have very low self-esteem and think that they deserve to be punished. Nothing could be farther from the truth. No one deserves that kind of punishment, least of all children. All children, whether very young or near adulthood (teens), need to be taught right from wrong, but hitting is not the way to do it. It hurts inside and out and perpetuates the cycle of pain to the following generations of children.

Sexual abuse is an even deeper, darker secret that is even harder to confess and harder to prove. As with physical abuse, the abusing parent was probably abused as a child, but that is no reason for letting the behavior continue. Often when the victim goes to the enabling parent there is shock and disbelief. He or she and even the abuser will say that you are lying. No one will believe you. But you must keep trying to get help, because otherwise you will continue to be abused.

In some states teachers, school counselors, doctors, and nurses are required by law to report cases of sexual abuse to the police. Sexual abuse of a minor is against the law, and the offender will be arrested and put in jail. If professionals do not report this crime, they can lose their license to practice or to teach in that state.

Often the family in a sexual abuse case may deny the abuse. The whole family may side with the abuser. You must not let them convince you that you are wrong, that it's your fault, or that you could have done something to prevent or stop it. It was not your fault. Your only hope is to keep telling everyone exactly what happened until you get at least one adult to help you take action. Then the truth will be known, and although the enablers resist admitting it, deep down they will know you are the victim of a terrible personal violation.

The whole family will need counseling if it is to remain

together. News of this kind can cause divorce and internal conflict for both children and adults. Not only psychological but physical changes must take place to repair the damaged family. Trust in the offending parent can only be reestablished gradually, but this healing process must take place if there is to be any hope for the family. The offending parent will be required to live elsewhere after he is released from jail so that he will never again have an opportunity to molest you.

If you are still afraid to report this crime to police or anyone who will have your parent arrested, you are not alone. Many children are in the terrible position of having to choose between their own mental health and happiness and having a parent suddenly dragged away by police. This nightmare is one that all abused children experience. They want the abuse to stop, yet they still love the offending parent. They are torn between love of self and love of another. All too often, with their own low self-esteem, they choose to keep silent to protect the offending parent.

We hope that after reading this book and others like it you will not sacrifice yourself for your parents. You have a life to lead, and you have the right to be safe and secure in your home. You should not feel forced or obligated to have sex with anyone, especially not a relative. It will leave you very confused and unhappy. Get help. Make them stop. No one can do it but you.

Emotional neglect is probably the most difficult to prove because the problem is not so much what the parent does as what he or she does *not* do—give love and attention. Your physical needs are met: You have food and shelter and clothing. But your parents are never there to talk with when something is bothering you. You know they are busy and your problems are not as important as theirs, or so you think. They give you no guidance with boyfriend/girlfriend problems. This type of abuse is most common with teenagers. Their parents are wrapped up in a career, and over the years they have made a habit of leaving their children with baby-sitters or at home alone. They meet their children's physical needs but they don't schedule time for them in their busy life. It is good for children to learn to be self-reliant and independent, but feeling isolated and alone is depressing for anyone regardless of age.

In all of these dysfunctional families, there is really only one person who can help you, and that is you. If you look around you in your home and it seems pretty clear that nothing is going to change, you have to decide how *you* will make it change. Decide what solution you want for the problem. Remember that it should be a solution that will not harm you any more than you have already been harmed. Ask yourself which is worse, living with the abuse or making things change? Other members of the family cannot help you, because they are suffering too. You are learning how to be your own parent. Care for yourself. That is not to say that your should be totally self-centered and insensitive to others, but you need to realize that the only one who can bring about a good change in your life is you.

It depends on your age when you read this, but essentially anyone from eleven to eighteen has several options. First, you need to take an overview of your life situation. Are you old enough to leave home and support yourself? Generally people in this age group find it difficult or impossible to support themselves earning minimum wage and working part time. So you would have to quit school and work full time. *Bad move.* Quitting school is the single *worst* thing you can do to change your life. School is probably not the real problem, so why deprive yourself of your only good ticket out of unhappy surroundings.

If you have come to the conclusion that you will try to stop the abuse by getting help—good for you, but you may need some protection yourself, especially in the case of physical abuse. If a child reports the crime and the parent is arrested but released on bond, the angry, out-of-control parent may try to get even by beating him or her worse than ever before. This child needs to tell the arresting officer that he or she wants to be put under court-ordered child protection.

Only you can decide if you want to take legal action to bring about a change in your dysfunctional family. Of course, it will disrupt your life too, but if you want to bring about a change once and for all and you can wait no longer, then do it. If you have a support person (teacher, neighbor, clergyperson), consult with him or her about your plan of action. Discuss other options. Then make your decision and *do it*. But be sure that you *know* what you are doing, that you have *realistically* planned how these changes are to take place, and that these changes will not destroy whatever shreds of a family are left.

Perhaps you have thought about it long and hard and have come to the conclusion that you will not be able to change the offending parents. Then what do you do? If you are between eleven and fifteen, leaving home is not a good idea. Teens rarely do well by leaving home and trying to be independent; it's just too expensive. If you must leave to maintain your own sanity, go into foster care until things improve at home. It would be wise to talk to your support person about your individual difficulties.

If you convince yourself that you can leave and find some kind of job—don't. Then you will fall into the "runaway" category and run the risk of being raped, robbed of what little money you get, or forced into prostitution like many unfortunate young people whose only home is the streets. Think, *think*, THINK before you make any move that will make your life *worse* and destroy any hope for a better future.

Perhaps you will realize that you can avoid being home at critical times by joining school clubs or groups (as in Vicki's story) or by doing odd jobs or baby-sitting that will give you a little financial freedom. These plus hitting the books, spending a lot of time in the library, and hanging on to friends are all things that you can effectively use to tune out what is happening at home.

However, if your personal safety is in danger at home, don't wait until you are eighteen to take action. Look in the Yellow Pages of your phone directory under "Crisis Intervention" and find a hotline number, or look in the Appendix. Give the person who answers all the facts in your situation, and he or she should be able to advise you on where and how to find safety. That way it remains private; you *do not* have to give your name.

If you are between fifteen and eighteen you have many more options. Again, don't drop out of school. That will hurt you. Try to find a job for weekends and summers. Restaurants are often good places to get started; they always seem to need help (perhaps because the pay is often only minimum wage). If you are a waiter or waitress, the tips put a great jingle in your pocket, and the whole work experience will give you confidence.

As you approach your senior year in high school, you will begin to consider leaving home. If you have kept up your studies you can apply for admission to a university or college. You don't need your parents' help for that and you should never let money problems stop you from attending college. Financial aid is available for anyone smart enough to apply for it: federal loans, grants, and scholarships, state financial aid, or even aid from your city. There are financial aid programs for certain subjects such as medicine and from groups such as veterans and religious groups. Try everything to pave the way, so that when you leave home you are not running *away* but running *to* something better.

You don't have to be a straight A student to go to college. Entrance requirements vary widely from state to state. Find out from the library or your guidance counselor how to apply for college entrance. It is wise to do this fairly early in your senior year so that you will be able to make plans. Apply to several schools so that if one does not accept you, another may. When you are accepted you will know that next fall you will live in a dorm, which will be much better than living with a dysfunctional family. You will have adjustments to make, naturally, but at least your personal safety will not be constantly threatened.

College is definitely worth the effort because of the countless career opportunities that it opens up. It will improve your prospects for the future both financially and personally. In college you will meet all kinds of kids. Some will be from normal families, showing you once again how messed up yours was by comparison. Some will be like you—from a dysfunctional family, and they did the same thing you did to escape.

On the other hand, if college is not the road you wish to pursue, then what? Upon graduation from high school many students begin job-hunting. Again you need to talk to your support person. Seek advice on what jobs you should apply for, which companies offer the best pay, which ones are currently hiring, which ones offer the best opportunities for advancement, or which are the closest to home if transportation is a problem.

You also need to decide whether to continue living at home or to find your own place? Do you have a friend to share an apartment with, to help to keep the cost down. You have many serious decisions to make about your short-term and long-term goals.

All this is very disturbing to think about, and sometimes it seems easier just to put it out of mind and ignore it. But that's what everyone else is doing, and things will never get any better that way. Think. Listen. Read. Talk to others. You are not alone unless you want to be. Many groups for dysfunctional families are forming all over the country. They are made up of people just like you, children, teens, and parents—all hurting just like you. They are very understanding and supportive. You are under no obligation to speak in these groups until you are ready and feel comfortable with the situation. It is only when you have come to grips with the past that you can take charge of the present and plan a brighter, happier, saner future for yourself and the family that you may someday create.

CHAPTER ◇ 9

Light at the End of the Tunnel—Your Future

We hope this book has shed some light on the problems of dysfunctional families. You can see now that dysfunction can take several forms. Each form is unique in its difficulties, but some feelings are common to all these groups. The result of all these kinds of abuse is the same. We share some or all of the emotions: guilt, low self-esteem, and anger. Of course everyone feels those emotions *sometimes*, but as a victim of abuse you have experienced much more of them than kids from normal families. You are accepting the fact that your home life has been very different and very unhealthy, both physically and mentally. You are struggling with all these feelings, and you need to know that you are not alone. In recent years psychologists and social workers have begun studying the family on all levels of our society. We need to understand how and why it works or doesn't work.

You recognize your own problems within your family, and now you are anxious to do something about them. In Chapter 8 we discussed the various options open to you and considered the consequences of your choice. Now we want to do a little predicting, based on studies of children from dysfunctional families. Although you wish to put your childhood behind you and get on with your future, you cannot. You will be haunted by memories that you have repressed for years, and those feelings will affect your everyday life. You may not even be aware of it at first. You know that something is wrong with the way you deal with other people and they react to you, but you can't put your finger on what it is. Some religious zealots would have us believe it is because we need more "god" in our lives. However, we choose to concentrate not on sin and death and the life (if any) after this one, but rather on the here and now, on a life full of joy and hope and beauty, a life worth living. Whatever your religious philosophy is, you are still a product of your environment, and that environment was unhealthy and disturbing. You need to learn more peaceful ways of communicating.

You experience a strong sense of loss for your own childhood and are probably very angry about it. Often we are taught to suppress our anger and not to demonstrate it in a socially unacceptable way (such as fighting, destroying things, or hurting other people or ourselves). We keep the anger in, and there it stays, just below the surface, ready to boil over. Then, when the anger finally shows itself, people don't understand where it came from. It seems unmotivated, like an overreaction. They never knew the feelings you held inside because you never told anyone. Maybe you aren't completely sure where the anger came from either. It frustrates you not to be able to control it.

You now have this anger and sadness over your sense of loss. Where did your childhood go? Why did you have all those problems while other kids didn't? Why don't your parents act like adults? *What did you do to deserve this?* That is where the guilt comes in. You begin to think that you are being punished for something. If only you could be more perfect these problems would go away. So you try to be good, better—the best kid you could possibly be. But no matter how hard you try, things don't improve. The abuse or neglect goes on.

Now you are very depressed and want to *blame* someone for all this pain. Whom do you blame? Your parents, for not caring for your needs? No. Your parents for their alcohol or drug abuse? No. Your enabling parent for allowing the problem to continue for so long? No. You blame—yourself. You blame yourself for what is happening and has happened in the past. You are full of self-criticism and self-doubt, and the feeling will act as a handicap in almost everything you do. In our highly competitive world, any degree of self-doubt can hurt career chances.

These are all feelings that, once recognized in yourself, you can work to overcome. All too often children from dysfunctional families spend half their life denying that they have a problem. They want all that unhappiness to stay securely locked up in the past. "It's over and done with. Let's get on with our lives," we say. As a teen *you* are realizing how and why you came to feel that deep, seemingly unmotivated, guilt and anger. If you understand where your feelings are coming from, it is easier to deal with them. That is not to say that you should whine and cry and wallow in self-pity. But you should understand that as a child of a dysfunctional family you have certain problems and weaknesses that others don't have.

In this life it is not so much what happens to you that matters as how you cope with it, how you react to it, that makes you who you are. A psychiatric nurse once told us that her experiences with troubled patients, many of them teens, has taught her that everyone has problems in this life. Some have them at the beginning of their life, some in the middle, and some at the end. But everyone has them. As a child of a dysfunctional family you have had your share of problems at the beginning of your life. Now it's up to you to build on what you have learned and try to overcome your handicaps so that the middle and end of your life can be lived in happiness and understanding of yourself and of those around you. As the Greek philosopher Socrates taught, "Know thyself." It is only with self-awareness that we can grow to our full potential. Know that you are full of anger and that it needs to be released in a constructive way. Know that you feel more guilty and self-critical than most people. You need to recognize your specific weaknesses before you can break their stranglehold on you and free yourself.

So far we have discussed only the emotional and psychological baggage you have gathered over the years. Now we shall discuss the physical weaknesses that you have inherited. Children of alcoholics are at risk of becoming alcoholics themselves. You know from watching other people drink that some people "just can't hold their liquor." They get drunker faster and at lower doses of alcohol than others. Why? Some seem unable to say no to a drink even when it is obvious that the party is over and there is no longer a need to drink "socially." Why? Is it because your brain chemistry may make you unable to fight off the disease of alcoholism? Or is it a question of metabolism? Or is it because you grew up in an environment saturated with drugs or alcohol and you see it as a good way to escape problems—a learned behavior?

Whether it is learned or you are born with it, the fact remains that children of alcoholics and drug abusers are more vulnerable themselves. The human body is a delicate and wonderful organism. When we experiment with drugs such as alcohol, cocaine, or marijuana we do not know what the result will be in our particular body. Some people can start and stop at will; others become slaves to the drug and endlessly seek to stimulate the pleasure center in their brain. Understand that as a child of an alcoholic you are four times more likely to become an alcoholic yourself. This is a physical disease that you can avoid now that you realize that you may carry a genetic weakness for alcoholism.

In sexual and physical abuse, the same hurtful behavior is repeated by adults who were abused. This is not a question of inheritance, but a learned behavior. Generation after generation has suffered with this problem. If you think that you might deal that way with your own children, get help before the hurting goes any further. A learned behavior can be unlearned and replaced with something better. You may think that you are too young to think about having children yourself. But learning parenting skills will enable you to communicate effectively with children or anyone else without using violence. Let your children be the first generation in your family to grow up without the hurt.

But remember, you cannot stop yourself without help. Seek professional help or join a group of others who have been similarly injured, so that you have some way of expressing all those hidden feelings of anger, guilt, and self-criticism. Join a group to learn better parenting skills, and just better living skills. Get help for the children of the future by getting help for yourself.

Okay, now you have a better understanding of the kind of mold you have been formed in. It is a place for secrets and hidden emotions. You know your predicted weaknesses based on research of others who have been brought up in dysfunctional families. Low self-esteem (too self-critical), a feeling of guilt (it's all your fault), and a deep and strong feeling of anger are the three most common and lasting effects of growing up in this chaos. What do you do? Where do you go from here?

Start with an assessment of yourself. What are your strengths? What are you good at? What do you value? What is important to you? Do you have any clear goals? What are your short-term goals (things you hope to do in the near future, such as get a job, leave home, become good at a certain sport)? What are your long-term goals (things you hope to do sometime in your life, for example, complete college, get married, have children, have a career, travel the world, own a home, earn a lot of money)?

Taking an inventory of your feelings about yourself and the world around you is a helpful method of clarifying your values. It can be private and for your eyes only. There are no right or wrong answers.

Get a sheet of paper and start by making a list of questions. The more varied, the better the overall picture you'll have of yourself. Start with some questions that can be answered with a simple yes, no, or maybe. For example:

1. Do you like holidays, like Christmas?
2. Have you ever had something stolen from you?
3. Can you type?
4. Do you like to read?

5. Do you hope to have children of your own someday?

Then your list can get more complicated and invite short answers. For example:

1. What are you most afraid of?
2. If you could change one thing about your parents, what would it be?
3. If you had a million dollars what would you spend it on?
4. If you could change one thing about yourself, what would it be?
5. What is your favorite color and what does it remind you of?

Don't stop with these sample questions. You will need to think of and answer many questions before you will begin to feel as though you know yourself better. Don't be afraid to come up with difficult questions, such as:

1. Do you think women should be given opportunity and advancement equal to men? What about equal pay?
2. If you were killed in an accident, would you want to have your organs donated?
3. What is your most valued personal freedom?
4. Do you think blacks should be given the same opportunities as whites?
5. When does life begin? At birth? At conception? Somewhere in between?
6. If you were ill and were being kept alive by machines, would you want them to "pull the plug"?

After completing your personal assessment inventory you may want to set it aside for a week or more. Then come back to it and read your answers again. Are you surprised at what you wrote, or does it still make sense? You are beginning to "know thyself." Remember that this is a lifelong process that is constantly changing. Ten years from now if you happen to run across this list in the bottom of your "junk" drawer, you will be amazed at the values that have changed and those that have remained the same. They make you who you are. They are important ideas and opinions because they are yours. No one else on this planet is exactly like you. Someday you will be called upon to act according to your beliefs. It's good to know what they are.

Realize that you are not your parents. You are a separate individual with different needs and desires. Ask yourself how you feel about many different things. You have probably been too busy surviving your family situation to really think about who you are and how you fit into the world. This search for identity does not end with this book. It is only the beginning of a lifetime of searching and growing and changing. Nothing is constant in this life except change, so we have to learn to be open to new ideas. However, growing up in a dysfunctional family has given you a sad view of personal relationships. You need to struggle with keeping your attitudes open and honest.

You are probably quite ready for a change and welcome it, but a change to what? Ask yourself how you will take control of your own life. What actions can you take that will help and in no way hurt you? Your past was in your parents' hands, and they had great difficulty being loving and caring parents. Your future is in your hands. What will you do with it? Will you rise above the problems and pressures of everyday living that troubled your parents? Are you resolved never to make the mistakes they did?

What is your plan for your life? Are your goals realistic? Are you doing anything now to make any of those dreams come true? You need to fight your feelings of worthlessness. You *can* make up your mind to do something and then do it. You are a survivor. All you need is a plan, a goal, a target. Aim high, because your guilt and self-criticism will try to pull you down. Build on the mistakes of others, and let your parents be an example of what *not* to become. Some kids have parents who give them encouragement and support. You have to do it for yourself. That doesn't make it impossible to achieve your goals, just a lot more challenging. People will respect and admire you more, knowing your background and realizing how far you've come. More important, *you* will respect and feel pride in yourself knowing that you have done it all, with little or no help from home. All your strength came from within. You must nurture and be good to yourself before you can be free to care for others. That is not to say that you should be conceited or arrogant, nor that you should use your childhood as a crutch or excuse for not doing anything with your life. Remember, sooner or later everyone has problems. In a way you are lucky: Yours came early, so now you can learn from the pain and hope to make things better for the later part of your life.

Let's look back at the outcomes of the dysfunctional families described in this book. In Chapter 1 we presented an overview of the subject of dysfunctional families in our society. Chapter 2 dealt with Alice's way of coping with her father's alcohol abuse. She described how she overcame this unhappy beginning and went on to a better life by continuing her education in college, which gave her a goal and an escape all in one.

In Chapter 3 Barry's coping abilities were not as strong. His mother's drug abuse affected him in such a way that psychiatric therapy was the only answer. His sister's suicide hurt and confused him deeply. She was no longer able to cope and chose to die. Barry's mother recognized the damage she had done to her children only after the shock of losing her daughter; she finally entered a therapy program. It was too late for her daughter, but she still has time to salvage her relationship with her son.

In Chapter 4 Roberto reacted to his father's violence by suppressing his anger so long that it finally erupted in a violent explosion.

He joined a street gang and in a moment of anger almost beat a man to death. Roberto's way of coping with his dysfunctional family was not successful. He ended up reflecting the image of his father in his violent behavior. Although we understand *why* Roberto acted as he did, we cannot condone his actions. They were a way of dealing with his surroundings that did not attempt to make his life better. His choices hurt himself and made his future look dim. He now has a police record and the court system to deal with. He only added to his problems by using violence to overcome violence.

Chapter 5 had to do with sexual abuse. In Tomika's story she did the only thing she could do to escape: She told someone what had happened. It took the shock of seeing her sister caught in the web of abuse to give her the courage to act. She felt very unhappy about having to tell on someone she loved, but she knew the abuse was spreading to her younger sister. Tomika's way of coping was by telling the truth and taking legal action against her father. Of course, she needed help from her friend's mother, but at least the nightmare was over.

Chapter 6 dealt with emotional neglect. Victoria's coping

method was to work hard to try to earn her parents' love and attention. She did not realize that her parents were probably unaware that a problem existed. Confrontation might have been a more successful way of letting her needs be known.

The way of coping with the dysfunctional family was different in each case, but the goal of all these teens was the same—to end the abuse and begin a better life. All five stories dealt with the victim's feelings of guilt, worthlessness, and anger. We hope that one or all of these stories helped you realize that you are not alone and that there are successful ways of coping with a dysfunctional family. It's all in your hands now. Only you can bring about change. Only you can give yourself a goal, a dream, a future.

Glossary

abuse   To mistreat, use wrongly, break.

crisis intervention   Emotional first aid for emergencies; can be over the phone, as a crisis intervention hotline.

drug   Chemical that causes the body to react; can be helpful, such as aspirin, or deadly, such as crack cocaine.

drug abuse   Overuse (which can mean *any* use) of stimulating or depressing drugs that affect the brain.

dysfunctional   Not working, broken, harmful.

emotional abuse   Neglecting to give love, safety; giving no praise or encouragement.

family therapy   Treatment of the whole family as a unit.

fondling   Touching sexual areas.

group therapy   Treatment of unrelated people with similar experiences, who try to help each other by listening and making suggestions to solve problems.

health care professional   Doctor, nurse, psychiatrist (who is an MD with special training and can prescribe medication for mental disorders such as clinical depression), psychologist, social worker, or psychiatric nurse.

incest   Sexual activity with a family member.

needs   Human requirements, from basic for the body (food, shelter) to higher (love, beauty) for the mind.

physical abuse   Hitting, kicking, cutting, pushing, or spanking; also failure to provide basics such as food, shelter, clothing.

pornography   Sexual photographs, books, or movies.

rape   Sexual penetration against the will of the victim.

sexual abuse   Kissing or touching in a way that makes you feel uncomfortable; fondling, showing pornography, being made to pose nude, intercourse with a minor by an adult.

Appendix

NATIONAL AND STATE CRISIS INTERVENTION HOTLINES

The following numbers are provided to make finding help easier for you. Remember that an 800 number is tollfree; all others are not. Local numbers may be listed in your telephone directory under "Crisis Intervention." If you are unable to reach a center near you, call your police department or emergency 911 number. If you feel suicidal, if your life is threatened, if you don't know where to turn, these hotlines may get you in touch with the help you need.

National Hotlines

Active Parenting, Atlanta, GA, 1-800-235-7755.
Alcohol and Drug Helpline, Salt Lake City, UT, 1-800-821-4357.
Alcoholism and Drug Addiction Treatment Center, La Jolla, CA, 1-800-382-4357.
ASAP Family Treatment of Chemical Dependency, Van Nuys, CA, 1-800-367-2727.
Brattleboro Retreat, VT, 1-800-345-5550.
Caron Foundation, Allentown, PA, 1-800-327-8878.
Community Hospital, Monterey, CA, 1-800-528-8080.
Family Assessment Consultation and Therapy Services, Fort Worth, TX, 1-800-537-2287.
Friary, Gulf Breeze, FL, 1-800-332-2271.
Gillette Abuse Refuge Foundation, Gillette, WY, 1-800-233-2965.
Glenbeigh Adult and Teen, Tampa, FL, 1-800-422-4643.

Harold Hughes Center, Des Moines, IA, 1-800-247-0764.

Insight, Flint, MI, 1-800-327-8989.

Johnson Institute, Minneapolis, MN, 1-800-231-5165.

Matagorda County Women's Crisis Center, Bay City, TX, 1-800-451-9235.

Massachusetts Cocaine Hotline, Woburn, MA, 1-800-822-0223.

Oakview Treatment Center, Ellicott City, MD, 1-800-223-7770.

Pacific Western Psychiatric Medical Group, Van Nuys, CA, 1-800-367-2727.

Pastoral Institute of Lagrange, Lagrange, GA, 1-800-527-1836.

Phoenix House Foundation, 1-800-532-4444.

PRIDE (Parents Resources Institute for Drug Education), 1-800-241-7946.

Rapides Regional Medical Center, Alexandria, LA, 1-800-367-3145.

Safe Recovery Systems, Atlanta, GA, 1-800-451-9355.

Sage Crossings, Plymouth, MA, 1-800-543-7243.

Saint Josephs Hospital Solutions Chemical Dependency Program, Alton, IL, 1-800-622-6213.

Schicks Shadel Hospital, Seattle, WA, 1-800-542-4202.

Valley of Hope Alcoholism and Drug Addiction Treatment Centers, 1-800-544-5101.

Whispering Pines Hospital, Keene, NH, 1-800-633-3633.

NATIONAL RUNNAWAY SWITCHBOARD, 1-800-621-4000.

State Hotlines

The following 800 listings are tollfree only for residents of the state.

Alabama	Birmingham, 205-323-7777.
Alaska	Anchorage, 907-279-7516.
Arkansas	Battered Women's Hotline, Little Rock, AR, 1-800-332-4443.
Arizona	Alcohol and Drug Recovery Center,

AZ 1-800-247-2322.
Phoenix, 602-258-6301.
Tempe, 602-968-2744.
Yuma, 602-783-5411.

California   Help Now Community Hospital of
                                Central California,
                                1-800-822-8448.
                                Bakersfield, 805-325-1232.
                                Berkeley, 415-548-2570.
                                Fresno, 209-485-1432.
                                Los Angeles, 213-620-0144.
                                Los Angeles, 213-435-7669.
                                Sacramento, 916-441-1138.
                                San Diego, 714-239-0325.
                                San Francisco 415-845-5470.

Colorado   Teen Hotline Durango,
                                1-800-221-8336.
                                Boulder, 303-449-5555.
                                Denver, 303-777-6619.
                                Denver, 303-746-8485.

Connecticut   Darien, 203-655-1485.
                                Middlebury, 203-758-1721.
                                New Haven, 203-787-2127.

Delaware   Wilmington, 302-758-5555.
District of Columbia   202-767-7221.
Florida   Jacksonville, 904-387-5641.
                                Miami, 305-633-7507.

Georgia   Atlanta, 404-892-1358.
                                Columbus, 404-324-HELP.

Hawaii   Honolulu, 808-521-4555.
Illinois   Chicago, 312-929-5150.
                                Des Plaines, 312-827-0440.
                                Evanston, 312-491-9125.
                                Peoria, 309-691-7373.

Indiana   Fort Wayne, 219-742-7333.
                                Indianapolis, 317-632-7575.

	Muncie, 317-289-0404.
	South Bend, 219-288-4842.
Iowa	Davenport, 319-322-1712.
	Dubuque, 319-556-4357.
	Waterloo, 319-556-4357.
Kansas	Garden City, 316-276-7689.
	Topeka, 913-235-3434.
	Wichita, 316-265-8577.
Louisiana	Baton Rouge, 504-388-1234.
Maine	Bangor, 207-946-6143.
	Portland, 207-775-3163.
Maryland	Baltimore, 301-523-2330.
	College Park, 301-454-HELP.
Massachusetts	Alcohol and Drug Referral Service,
	800-327-5000.
	Boston, 617-599-1739.
	Cambridge, 617-492-2000.
	Lowell, 617-256-5488.
	New Bedford, 617-997-7777.
	Quincy, 617-471-7100.
Michigan	Ann Arbor, 313-761-HELP.
	Detroit, 313-875-5466.
	East Lansing, 517-337-1717.
	Grand Rapids, 616-682-4234.
Minnesota	Minneapolis, 612-339-7033.
	St Paul, 612-225-1515.
Mississippi	Meridian, 601-693-1001.
Missouri	Kansas City, 816-471-3000.
	St. Joseph, 816-232-1655.
	St. Louis, 314-721-1517.
Montana	Battered Women's Network,
	Bozeman, 800-225-9789.
	Billings, 406-245-6424.
Nebraska	Lincoln, 402-472-7211.
	Omaha, 402-536-6749.
Nevada	Reno, 702-323-6111.

New Hampshire	Child and Family Service of New Hampshire, Manchester, 800-642-6486.
	Hanover, 603-646-1110.
	Helpline, 800-992-3312.
New Jersey	Orange, 201-673-0636.
	Pompton Plains, 201-696-6633.
	Teaneck, 201-692-1500.
New Mexico	Albuquerque, 505-255-1674.
New York	Drug Abuse Hotline, 800-538-4840.
	Drug Abuse Information, 800-522-5353.
	Albany, 518-465-4149.
	Brooklyn, 212-462-3322.
	Buffalo, 716-854-6555.
	Ithaca, 607-272-1616.
	New York, 212-777-4880.
	Schenectady, 518-377-8119.
North Carolina	Charlotte, 704-333-6121.
	Durham, 919-688-5504.
	Greenville, 919-758-HELP.
North Dakota	Bismarck, 701-255-4124.
	Fargo, 701-232-4357.
Ohio	Akron, 216-535-5181.
	Cincinnati, 512-621-2273.
	Columbus, 614-294-6378.
Oklahoma	Alcohol Training and Education, 800-522-9050.
	Lawton, 405-355-7575.
	Help in Crisis Regional Hotline, 800-343-5763.
Oregon	Eugene, 503-344-7133.
	Portland, 503-228-4357.
Pennsylvania	Helpline, Willamsport, 800-624-4636.

	Erie, 814-453-5656.
	Lancaster, 717-393-1715.
	Philadelphia, 215-546-7766.
	Pittsburgh, 412-682-5200.
Rhode Island	Providence, 401-461-4673.
South Carolina	Greenville, 803-239-1021.
South Dakota	Mitchell, 605-996-6696.
Tennessee	Battered Women Inc., Crossville, 800-641-3434.
	Memphis, 901-525-1717.
	Nashville, 615-329-9016.
Texas	Austin, 512-478-5657.
	Corpus Christi, 512-883-6244.
	Dallas, 214-369-1008.
	San Antonio, 512-734-5726.
Utah	Provo, 801-375-5111.
Virginia	Alexandria, 705-548-3810.
	Richmond, 703-359-3257.
Washington	Bellingham, 206-734-7271.
	Seattle, 206-325-5550.
West Virginia	Charleston, 304-346-4444.
Wisconsin	Eau Claire, 715-834-1212.
	Madison, 608-257-3522.
	Milwaukee, 414-271-3123.
Wyoming	Sexual Assault and Family Violence Task Force, Evanston, 1-800-445-7233.
	Cheyenne, 307-634-4469.
	Powell, 307-754-5121.

Places to Write for More Information

Children of Alcoholics Foundation Inc.
54 Madison Avenue
New York, NY 10022

National Institute on Drug Abuse
P.O. Box 2305
Rockville, MD 20852

Alateen & Al-Anon Family Group
1372 Broadway
New York, NY 10018-0862

Incest Survivors Anonymous
P.O. Box 5613
Long Beach, CA 90800

Johnson Institute
510 First Avenue North
Minneapolis, MN 55403-1607

Multi-Cultural Prevention Work Group
429 Forbes Avenue
Pittsburgh, PA 15219
(Information on substance abuse among Native Americans and
other minorities)

National Association for Children of Alcoholics
P.O. Box 421961
San Francisco CA 94142

National Clearinghouse for Alcohol Information
P.O. Box 2345
Rockville MD 20853

National Council on Alcoholism
12 West 21st Street
New York, NY, 10010

Suggested Reading

ALCOHOLISM

Black, Claudia. *It Will Never Happen to Me: Children of Alcoholics*. MAC Publishing, 1982.

Hornick, Edith. *You and Your Alcoholic Parent*. Associated Press, 1974.

Leite, Evelyn, and Pamela Espeland. *Different Like Me*; a book for teens who worry about their parents' use of alcohol/drugs. Johnson Institute Books, 1987.

Woititz, Janet. *Adult Children of Alcoholics*. Health Communications, 1983.

PHYSICAL ABUSE

Miller, Alice. *Thou Shalt Not Be Aware: Society's Betrayal of the Child*. New American Library, 1986.

Pagelow, Mildred Daley. *Family Violence*, Prager Publishing, 1984.

SEXUAL ABUSE

Angelou, Maya, *I Know Why the Caged Bird Sings*. Bantam, 1980.

Ledray, Linda. *Recovery from Rape*. Holt, 1986.

Maltz, Wendy, and Beverly Holman. *Incest and Sexuality: A Guide to Understanding*. Lexington Books, 1987.

DRUG ABUSE

Bartimole, Carmella and John. *Teenage Alcoholism and Substance Abuse*. Fredrick Fell Publishers, 1987.
Schaefer, Dick. *Choices and Consequences*. Johnson Institute, 1987.

Index